CRAFTING COLLECTIVITY

CRAFTING COLLECTIVITY

AMERICAN RAINBOW GATHERINGS AND ALTERNATIVE FORMS OF COMMUNITY

CHELSEA SCHELLY

THANK YOU

Chelsea Schelly

Paradigm Publishers

Boulder • London

Copyright © 2015 Paradigm Publishers

Published in the United States by Paradigm Publishers, 5589 Arapahoe Avenue, Boulder, CO 80303 USA.

Paradigm Publishers is the trade name of Birkenkamp and Company, LLC, Dean Birkenkamp, President and Publisher.

Library of Congress Cataloging-in-Publication Data
Schelly, Chelsea.
    Crafting collectivity : American rainbow gatherings and
alternative forms of community / Chelsea Schelly.
        pages   cm
    Includes bibliographical references and index.
    ISBN 978-1-61205-746-0 (pbk. : alk. paper)
    1. Rainbow Family of Living Light. 2. Utopias—United States. 3. Communities—United States. 4. Alternative lifestyles—United States. I. Title.
    HX806.S2548   2014
    307.77—dc23
2014012172

Printed and bound in the United States of America on acid-free paper that meets the standards of the American National Standard for Permanence of Paper for Printed Library Materials.

18 17 16 15 14   1 2 3 4 5

To baby, and Avery, and the Family.

CONTENTS

ACKNOWLEDGMENTS

This book would not have been possible without the support and encouragement of three particular academic mentors. Professor Jean Blocker at the University of Tulsa was the first person to inspire my sociological imagination and the first professor to suggest that I participate in Rainbow Gatherings as a sociological observer. To her, I must say thank you, thank you for believing in my capabilities as a sociologist at the very beginning stages of their development. Professor Peter Taylor at Colorado State University encouraged me to study people who were using technologies in alternative ways to pursue alternative lifestyles, recognizing this as my passion and prompting me to pursue that passion, even when I was timid about it. Thank you, Pete, for nurturing my intellectual enthusiasm and nourishing my personal drive to study and pursue alternatives that benefit the natural world and social relationships. Mustafa Emirbayer at the University of Wisconsin–Madison, my PhD advisor, recommended quite directly that I study and write about Rainbow Gatherings after he learned about my interest and involvement. Without his support, this book would not have come to fruition. His courses on sociological theory and the Chicago school of sociology intro-duced me to a sociological tradition that resonates with my own perspective and interest. His mentoring guided my approach, reminding me of what to watch for and how to stay attentive. His own enthusiasm for the project helped keep me energized. His tireless editing, of this project and many others, has drastically improved my written work. To him, I express my deepest gratitude: without you, this book would not have been possible.

There are several other people who made this book possible who also deserve much thanks and appreciation. Thank you to the three young men from Tulsa,

Oklahoma, who introduced me to Rainbow Gatherings. Thank you to my partner in life, who has made this dream and many other dreams come true. He attended the 2012 National Gathering with me, taking responsibility for the driving and our dogs, making my long days of extensive field research possible. He has spent considerable time listening to me talk about this project and reading drafts of this manuscript and has always been willing to discuss ideas or share his own experiences. Without his love and support, I would not be where I am today, and this book would not be here either. Thanks to Butterfly Bill for writing his own personal accounts of experiences at Gatherings over the past twenty years, which taught me much about Rainbow Family history, for taking the time to provide extensive feedback on a draft of this manuscript, and for dedicating so much positive energy to the Family. I must also say thank you to my family, who have encouraged and supported my educational journey, and to the Rainbow Family, who have allowed me to learn from them and inspired me in so many ways. This book is for all those who have taught me about the possibilities of freedom, for anyone who knows someone who has been drawn into this world and is wondering about its mysterious appeal, and for everyone who believes that the social and material configuration of our current world is not the only possibility. Finally, I must thank Dean Birkenkamp at Paradigm Publishers for believing in this project.

INTRODUCTION

It was during my first year at college that I learned about Rainbow Gatherings and the Rainbow Family of Living Light. At seventeen years old, I—like many Americans around that age—had just moved to a new place and was searching for new people, experiences, and ways of life that seemed a better fit for me than what my childhood upbringing had offered. I had already declared my sociology major when I attended my first Gathering, and I have since gone to six National Gatherings as both participant and observer, using sociological insight to understand the Rainbow Family and their Gatherings.

Rainbow Gatherings are temporary events that take place in National Forests throughout America, and those who attend identify as the Rainbow Family of Living Light. This family is a society of "fission-fusion"[1]—an ephemeral collection of people, material systems, and cultural practices that come together and are established, maintained, and then completely dismantled and "disappeared" only to take shape in another location, again and again, year after year.

Rainbow Gatherings are based on "principles of nonviolence and nonhierarchical egalitarianism."[2] The Rainbow Family has gathered every summer since 1972 "to pray for world peace and to demonstrate the viability of a cooperative utopian community living in harmony with the Earth."[3] Decisions are made by consensus in councils, which are open to all gatherers. Gatherings are completely noncommercial; there is no entrance fee and all necessities of life are provided for free. At a Gathering, "Everyone is welcome."[4] One way the Rainbow Family expresses its complete inclusivity is through the maxim that "everyone with a belly button"[5] is welcome, is home, at a Gathering.

This is a study of a very specific and somewhat unusual countercultural happening in America, a unique social world with its own vocabulary, economic structure, material systems, means of organizing, cultural customs, and practices. The elements of this social world shape the kinds of action and interaction that happen within it.[6] A unique blend of spirituality, anarchy, back-to-the-land living systems, and a leave-no-trace environmental ethic come together as thousands of people gather to party, pray, and experience the heightened sense of connectivity that takes place in this unusual social world. Yet the questions raised and insights offered by examining the world of the Rainbow Family provide more generally applicable insight into how the material organization of our society affects how we organize culturally and how the material and technological systems that support human societies also shape thought, action, and interaction.

Rainbow Gatherings are different from mainstream American society in numerous fundamental ways; they are organized differently both materially and culturally, and they involve different kinds of action and interaction. Some people are attracted to studying deviant groups because they offer "the promise of excitement or the exotic."[7] Yet, as sociologist Howard Becker suggests, deviance is just another form of collective action and "the field of deviance is nothing special, just another kind of human activity to be studied and understood."[8] What we consider deviant—whether it's smoking marijuana, walking around the woods naked, living without money, or sharing meals and freely exchanging hugs with strangers—is defined for us by society. We all "learn through social interaction to interpret"[9] and assign meaning to our physical experiences. Thus, at a Rainbow Gathering, just like in the rest of society, people learn from one another how to behave and how to interact; further, in both this alternative community subculture and in our mainstream culture, the ways we organize the materials, technologies, and physical systems that provide for subsistence and comfort reinforce particular cultural expectations regarding our actions, interactions, and social organization.

Social Worlds, Interaction, and Ritual: Approach and Arguments

In this book I examine Rainbow Gatherings as a social world. The idea of social worlds and the approach to studying them was originally used by scholars associated with the Chicago school of sociology, a dominant institution and unique bundle of ideas, perspectives, and methods born during the 1920s attentive to how spatial organization shapes social organization and how both influence the forms and patterns of human interaction. Many of the works by Chicago school sociologists concentrate on the study of social worlds, spaces in which unique forms of social organization and symbolic meanings arise to shape shared rules, behaviors, practices, language, and conceptions of morality.[10] From the taxi-dance hall[11] to the Chinese laundry man,[12] early ethnographies from the Chicago school tradition focus on the practices, interactions, and constructions of meaning that take place within what they call social worlds. Authors from the Chicago school describe social worlds as interactional spaces, with peculiar forms of contextually situational processes and specific forms of organization that shape behavior and understandings of meaning.

Anselm Strauss, who has more recently elaborated on the concept of a social world, writes, "In each social world, at least one primary activity (along with related clusters of activity) is strikingly evident. . . . There are sites where activities occur: hence space and a shaped landscape are relevant. Technology (inherited or innovative modes of carrying out the social world's activities) is always involved. Most worlds evolve quite complex technologies."[13] As a social world, the Rainbow Family of Living Light has "its own ways of acting, talking, and thinking. It has its own vocabulary, its own activities and interests, its own conception of what is significant in life, and—to a certain extent—its own scheme of life."[14] Rainbow Gatherings are a unique social world with their own forms of spatial, social, and material organization, unique technologies, and shaped landscapes as well as shared language, activities, and a holistic "scheme of life" that influences the kinds of action, interaction, and conceptualizations of meaning that take place within them.

Sociologist Andrew Abbott once argued that, for Chicago school sociologists, organization "meant 'the organizing of social life': a gerund rather than a noun, a process rather than a thing."[15] Sociologists from the Chicago school envisioned "society in terms of groups and interaction rather than in terms of independent individuals with varying characteristics"[16] and they paid particular attention to how social organization develops through dynamic interaction within a spatial and temporal context. In other words, Chicago school sociologists asked questions about the spatial patterns that arise, through interaction, to shape processes of social organization.

Attentiveness to the processes of organization as well as the interactions that take place within the social world of a Rainbow Gathering demonstrates the connections between its material and cultural structures. The technologies of a Gathering—the ways its participants physically organize their world and meet their needs of subsistence and comfort through material systems—is based upon the unique culture and the shared practices, experiences, interactions, and understandings at a Gathering. The organization of material structures simultaneously reinforces and contributes to Rainbow Gathering culture.

While the Chicago school of sociology provides a useful method and approach for studying social worlds, this study of Rainbow Gatherings also draws upon work from two earlier sociologists interested in questions of culture and connectivity: Emile Durkheim and his protégé Marcel Mauss. Their examinations of material culture and cultural ritual can also help us understand the actual happenings at a Rainbow Gathering. Specifically, this unique social world provides an excellent example of what Durkheim called *collective effervescence*, in which rituals and a shared demarcation of the sacred help to bring about a temporarily intensified sense of collective identity and communal sentimentality.

Durkheim used the term *collective effervescence* to describe moments of heightened social connectivity, emotional experiences in which sense of self dissipates into a more profound feeling of connection, like the out-of-body "highs" sometimes created by an expressive church service, a large rock concert or music festival, or a good support group meeting. The structure and organization of the material systems that support life at a Gathering shape the culture of this social world and both material and cultural organization help to craft a sense of collective effervescence, an air of "emotional intensity, a highly charged atmosphere of passionate involvement in everything."[17]

Marcel Mauss studied Eskimos[18] to understand how cultural expressions during times of collective experience are shaped by the material systems and material organization of a social group. Like the Rainbow Family, life among the Eskimos was marked by a distinct and recurring temporal rhythm, where changes in the material organization of life correspond to profound shifts in the cultural experience. The material and cultural systems of a Rainbow Gathering, like the physical and social organization of Eskimo society, together help to craft the profound sense of social connection often experienced by those who temporarily gather.

Relying on Durkheim and sociological work inspired by his thought, we can consider Rainbow Gatherings as a unique form of ritual:[19] open to all (and to all interpretations); entirely antidogmatic (although there are some cultural norms); acted out in the "cathedral of nature"; and involving open, participatory, and free for all forms of technological implementation appropriate to the specific physical location and the unique cultural system. This social world, which "opens up to you, accepts you, and invites you in,"[20] involves forms of both material and cultural ritual that contribute to the heightened sense of connectivity experienced by many of the participants.

Marcel Mauss, who sought to understand how material forms of organization contribute to social ritual and collective experience, wrote that some sociological investigations "are intended not just to describe but also to elucidate the material substratum of societies."[21] By *material substratum* he meant the "individuals who compose the society, the way in which they occupy the land, and the nature and configuration of objects of every sort which affect collective relations," and he believed that the "constitution of this substratum affects, directly or indirectly, all social phenomena."[22] Durkheim used the term *social morphology* to indicate the importance of the material world for understanding social organization and social experience. The character of both our private and our collective, social life shapes and is shaped by our material world and the way we use and interact with the physical environment around us to (in Strauss's terms) carry out our activities within our world, including all of the uncountable ways in which we modify the world into technological systems and structures from automobiles to private subdivisions to electricity to trailer parks. The material substratum shapes the organization of our social life, the associated constructed social meanings, and the culture in which we think, act, and interact.

Mauss set out to study "how the material form of human groups—the very nature and composition of their substratum—affects different modes of collective activity."[23] Here, I carry on with this aim, seeking to understand how the unique material organization affects how people act and interact within the distinctive collective life of a Rainbow Gathering. Durkheim and Mauss as well as others such as anthropologist Victor Turner[24] and contemporary sociologist Randall Collins[25] lend great insight into how material systems and social organization reinforce one another to craft an elevated sense of emotional connectivity when the social collective fuses and is internalized through a heightened ritual experience.

Chicago school sociology, which was itself indebted to Emile Durkheim's work, offers an approach to sociological study that provides fresh insight on ideas about ritual and collective effervescence. The emphasis on social worlds in Chicago school sociology is consistent with the earlier cultural sociology of Durkheim, one of the discipline's key founders, and it offers both an approach and a method to understanding the cultural phenomenon that so interested the French thinker.[26] The approach focuses on the actions and interactions of real people in real space, on spatial organization and the processes through which it develops, and on the specifics of the social world's emergent and evolving culture. The method is ethnographical, focusing on the lives and bodily experiences of humans interacting within a specific space and time. These tools allow us to understand particular forms[27] of cultural ritual, a topic that has interested sociologists since the earliest days of the discipline.

More specifically, Chicago school sociology reminds us that action and interaction are key and that both are spatially and contextually contingent. Durkheim did not explicitly share the Chicago school's focus on interaction involving physical, bodily movement and gestures as well as verbal and nonverbal forms of communication as the locus of social existence. Understanding the importance of interaction in both analysis and explanation came to sociology later than Durkheim, in the work of the Chicago school and other sociologists who were interested in small-scale and cultural questions, such as Erving Goffman and Georg Simmel.[28] Goffman believed that interaction was a natural unit for sociological study,[29] while Simmel claimed that interaction is the primary and most significant sociological unit of analysis[30] and even defined society itself as nothing more than interaction among individuals.[31]

Finally, the Chicago school and later sociologists working within its tradition emphasize the cultural aspects of social organization while being attentive to space, spatial context, and spatial organization (as Marcel Mauss was before them). The Chicago tradition reminds sociologists that physical space and spatial arrangement are important for understanding the social world. Furthermore, both come about through processes of physical human action and interaction. Accordingly, my work is explicitly observant of spatial organization and spatial context. Attentiveness to processes of social organization demonstrates how space is itself an important aspect of ritual and how spatial context can contribute to the experience of collective effervescence as well as our sociological understandings of it.

My methodological approach and sociological inspirations, as outlined above, mean that certain aspects of the Rainbow Family and their Gatherings are emphasized here while others are given less attention than they arguably deserve.[32] The chapters and the stories within them focus on two primary aspects of life at a Rainbow Gathering. The first is the material structures that facilitate dwelling at a Gathering—the free food provision and distribution; the temporary water supply systems; construction and maintenance of sanitary facilities; the freely provided health care and medical treatment; the organization of the physical environment—these are the tangible, physical things that make Gatherings happen. The second is the bodily action and personal interaction that take place at a Rainbow Gathering. I have often pondered the relationship between the two, how the technological structures that support human dwelling are shaped by and come to shape how we act and interact with one another, and this question underlies my presentation and discussion of the Rainbow Family and their Gatherings.

Examining Rainbow Gatherings as a social world with an ethnographic attentiveness to spatial arrangements, processes of organization, and rituals of interaction allows me to make several general arguments of a theoretical, substantive, and normative nature. Theoretically, I argue that the material systems that support personal life (such as those that provide energy, water, food, and a means of treating waste) influence the form and character of social life. At a Rainbow Gathering, free and openly accessible material systems contribute to the free and open social life and experience. Further, material systems are imbued in forms of ritual experience, and there is a benefit to being attentive to material forms and material organization when studying ritual. Other sociologists have occasionally acknowledged the relationship between material structures and cultural systems, as Marcel Mauss did when studying the Eskimo[33] and Georg Simmel did when examining urban life.[34] Yet we often forget how profoundly our material surroundings, including the technological systems we use to meet our subsistence needs and the ways we organize these systems, affect our social structures, cultural understandings, and means of interacting with one another.

A second theoretical argument is that collective effervescence doesn't just happen. Moments of temporarily heightened emotional connectivity with the social group are crafted through the participation and, most importantly, interaction, of human beings with one another and with their social world. Other sociologists, including Erving Goffman,[35] have focused on the importance of interaction rituals in understanding the social experience, and Goffman is said to be applying Durkheim at the micro level of social interaction to understand how interaction produces and reinforces moral solidarity.[36] Here, I explicitly highlight the importance of interaction as key for understanding how these temporary moments of social exaltation, in their many different forms, are crafted through the collective participation of individuals. "Social worlds which communicate and furnish relevance to social actors do not simply happen, or come as pre-packaged self-contained units"[37]—the creation of a crafted social identity and collective experience happens through interaction.

Substantively, this examination of a unique social world allows us to more fully understand our own participation in social worlds. The ways you interact with your sports team or church group are not natural or inevitable; they are social experiences full of their own constructions of language, appropriate forms of interaction, and accepted standards of normal behavior (all co-constituted within the material and technological organization of the social world). Although the social world of a Rainbow Gathering may seem strange or unusual to you, it is no more or less socially constructed than your own social worlds. A framework focused on interaction illustrates "how social actors define each other and their environments"[38] in the context of bodily behavior and the real and perceived responses to that behavior; our own behaviors and shared understandings of normal behavior are shaped by the interactions we have with both the organization of material objects and other social beings.

A second substantive argument is that contradictions threatening the ritual experiences of collective effervescence within this social world can actually, albeit precariously, be used to reinforce that same collective sentiment. At a Rainbow Gathering, rituals of freedom work to enroll contradictory people and practices in general collective sentiments and forms of expression. Not all participants at a Rainbow Gathering adhere to all of the organizational and social values of the Rainbow Family (such as active participation, nonviolent behavior, and openly kind interaction). However, the presence of contradictory people and actions actually contributes to the heightened sense of collectivity felt by other participants because the key value and practice of a Gathering is freedom. This freedom is qualified; exploitation of nature or other humans and the use of direct physical violence against another are never acceptable actions at a Gathering. Yet the freedom to act and interact in any way that does not impinge upon the rights of others to do the same is a key facet in enrolling individuals in a collective sense of social life at a Gathering, a social life in which participants experience a truer form of liberty through their sense of togetherness.[39]

Other groups wishing to sustain a heightened sense of collectivity—from support groups to religious organizations to social movements seeking mobilization and protest—may learn from this example and seek to find ways of using even potential contradictions to reinforce collective sentiments. The reality of a Rainbow Gathering does not match any picturesque or ideal image of complete peace, perfect love, or full cooperation. But the tensions and ambiguities that arise in this social world teach us something about how contradictions can, and sometimes do, make reality more real—and more sustainable over time.

Examining the long history of Rainbow Gathering culture, we can also consider substantive questions regarding this sustainability, regarding longevity and change over time. While I must admit that many aspects of the so-called hippie counterculture of the 1960s and 1970s (a broad category indeed) appeal to me both sensibly and emotively, Rainbow Gatherings are not simply a remnant of the hippie era, although they certainly began as an event firmly rooted in the 1960s counterculture. Many of the people who attend Gatherings do not look like or act like hippies. The diversity of value systems, priorities, and worldviews among Rainbow Gathering participants makes sustaining this social world a distinct challenge; yet gatherers continue to gather. By finding ways to embrace the ambiguities and contradictions as well as the demographic and cultural changes over time as part of the Gathering experience, the Rainbow Family provides insight into sustaining a social world even in the face of change.

Normatively, this study allows us to get up close and personal with an unusual, countercultural group of people, opening our minds to new conceptions of what is possible and desirable in terms of how we organize society both materially and culturally. The theoretical argument regarding the influence of material technologies on social organization and personal practice raises the question: What social forms do the material structures of mainstream American society support, and what tendencies in social organization do we wish to promote through the material systems that support residential life?

More specifically, it is my hope that examining this unique social world will raise questions like: How should we meet the material needs and comforts of individuals in society? How do different ways of doing so lead to different ways of acting and interacting, and what kinds of social interaction and social organization do we want to encourage through the material systems we adopt? What can we learn from this unique social world to help us understand our own times, our own culture, and our own ambitions for where we go from here?

A Note on Privilege

Admittedly, many of those who participate in Rainbow Gatherings—attending regional Gatherings in their home state or the annual American National Gathering—do not share my educational background. I say this to acknowledge that my presentation here is influenced not only by the perspectives and tools given to me through my sociological training but also by the perceptions lent to me by my social conditions. Seeing this as both an opportunity and a crutch, I recognize that my sociological view as shared herein is innately colored by the material and cultural world I inhabit,[40] shaped by the expectations brought by my education. I write from this position and while dwelling deeply within the interests I have developed throughout my sociological training.

Even though I started attending Gatherings as just another human with a belly button (not an academic researcher) and consider Rainbow Gatherings one of my homes on this Earth, I am what sociologist Georg Simmel would describe as a stranger[41] within the Rainbow Family: I am a part of it and yet I stand outside of it. I identify with it but also can't help standing back to analyze it.[42]

My position of stranger-ness within the Rainbow Family could be seen as an asset; Simmel says that the social distance of the stranger provides a greater freedom and that this freedom allows for greater objectivity.[43] Nevertheless, I must acknowledge that my position as a stranger is at least partially created by the habits, tastes, practices, and preferences I've learned based on my educational and social position in Babylon (how people in the Rainbow Family refer to all of society outside of a Rainbow Gathering). Sociologist Pierre Bourdieu used the term *habitus*[44] to capture the habits, tastes, practices, and preferences that we learn and internalize as part of our location in metaphorical social space, based on the experience we accrue in our particular class and status positions. People with different levels of educational attainment and people of different standings in class and status utilize the tools of their *habitus* to culturally reinforce and perpetuate their position in society. In other words, "A status, a position, a social place is not a material thing, to be possessed and then displayed; it is a pattern of appropriate conduct, coherent, embellished, and well articulated."[45] My own *habitus,* different from many of those who attend Rainbow Gatherings, influences how I experience this unique social world and shapes what I write about (and how) in ways that I recognize and probably in many other ways that I do not.

I hesitantly suggest that most readers of this book may inhabit a social milieu closer to Chelsea the Sociologist than Chelsea the Rainbow Sister. Some aspects of the Rainbow Family's social world may shock or surprise you, but I urge you to ask yourself how this fringe social world may tell you something about your own embodied experiences, and perhaps spend an extra second pondering these possibilities at the moments when these stories seem most shocking. After all, "The most barbarous and the most fantastic rites and the strangest myths translate some human need, some aspect of life, either individual or social. The reasons with which the faithful justify them may be, and generally are, erroneous; but the true reasons do not cease to exist."[46]

The Nitty-Gritty

Every year, the Rainbow Family of the Living Light holds an annual National Gathering. Although I have attended six of these Gatherings since 2002, only in 2012 did I attend explicitly for research purposes. Thus, most of what is presented here comes from that Gathering, although these stories are shared based on several years of experience suggesting their commonality and relevance. Although there are regional Rainbow Gatherings across the country all year long (so that some people spend the entire year "on the Rainbow trail," living a nomadic existence as they travel from Gathering to Gathering) as well as Gatherings throughout the world (including International and World Gatherings as well as regional and National Gatherings in other countries), here I focus specifically on the American National Rainbow Gathering that officially takes place in a different National Forest every year during the first week of July (although people are there long before and after that week) and has occurred annually since 1972. Rainbow Gatherings offer a classic example of collective effervescence in the modern world, as people from all walks of life experience a heightened sense of connectivity, collectivity, and social identity in this temporary metropolis in the woods.

Rainbow Gatherings are ephemeral; they are temporary Gatherings of people who are in the same place at the same time, practicing some of the same forms of material and cultural ritual. The unique ways of organizing materially and interacting culturally contribute to an emotively heightened sense of connectivity, a sense of collective effervescence, for many of the people who participate.

It is a common Rainbow Family aphorism that "no one speaks for the Rainbow Family." This phrase applies as much to me, a researcher attempting to illustrate some aspects of the Family and their Gatherings, as to anyone else who's attended Rainbow Gatherings. The Rainbow Family is adamantly not an organization. There are no official leaders, elected or otherwise. There is no membership list. No one knows everyone who's in the Family, and no one could say that someone's definitively in or out. Anyone and everyone who comes to a Gathering accomplishes all of the physical, organizational, and emotional work that goes into making a Rainbow Gathering happen, and everyone has a unique experience and an individual perception of that experience.

Like many sociological ethnographers who have come before me,[47] I seek to tell it like it is, sharing the bodily and emotional experiences of myself and others as we dwell in the social world of the Rainbow Gatherings with all those who gather. Butterfly Bill, one longtime participant in the Rainbow Family, has published two memoir accounts of his experiences at the National Rainbow Gatherings since 1987, and his stories serve as important references and validity checks for my own work.[48] Since I am studying Rainbow Gatherings as a social world, I am interested in their overall organization, the material systems that support them, the forms of communication and interaction that take place within them, and general cultural processes and expressions that arise in this particular space. Thus, the narrative presented here is in some ways different from a typical ethnography that focuses on a very minute examination of a very small group of individuals.[49] The vast majority of this writing is based directly on empirical accounts from firsthand experience, and it is shared through long descriptions and recounting stories in the first person. Each chapter will conclude with a short pause from this more descriptive narrative to conceptually grapple with the themes unveiled through the tales.

For all those with a belly button: Welcome home.

Chapter 1
What's with That Rainbow Fest?

Sitting at Carefree Cafe, the only twenty-four-hour coffee shop in Tulsa, Oklahoma, I stare idly at my economics homework, wishing I hadn't already finished my sociology reading for the week. A freshman in college, I still have the teenage drive to try to look older than I am—I am chain-smoking cigarettes and don the unusual combination of a shaved head and a long polyester dress printed with large bright flowers. Neither makes me stand out in this place where everything and everyone are (or maybe are just trying to be) alternative, different, unusual, against the mainstream—everything I wanted to explore after my suburban upbringing.

It was that night, after my schoolbooks had been put away, that my world changed. That night, I met Cadence, Jack, and Sam. Cadence and Jack were just a few years older than me and went to the community college in town. Sam was older, in his mid-thirties; to me, his eyes held all the wisdom in the world.

It was late spring, already after spring break, and for a college student there's often nothing left to talk about at that time of year except summer. So our conversation quickly turned to the season of freedom for those with a semester-based schedule, and they told me where they were headed.

"To the Rainbow Gathering," Cadence told me.

"Rainbow what?" I asked, trying not to sound too naïve.

"A Rainbow Gathering. It's basically where a bunch of hippies come together and hang out in the woods. Everything's free, I mean all the food and stuff, and it's always a good time. I mean, what's better than free living in the woods? And the people are so cool. It's like a big party."

So at the end of May 2002, I traveled to my first Rainbow Gathering with Cadence, Jack, and Sam. It was the Oklahoma regional Gathering, and we rode together in Cadence's old Subaru with faux-wood paneling, the piles of camping gear overflowing from the station wagon's rear storage compartment and cramping those of us seated in the back.

What Is a Rainbow Gathering?

Driving to the Oklahoma regional Gathering that summer was an eye opener: I didn't even know that there were roads in America so worn and potholed, and certainly couldn't comprehend that I would drive many more similar roads in the coming decade. We drove for miles down a seemingly endless dirt Forest Service road before coming to the "front gate," where an old man with sorrowful eyes kindly gave us directions to park and walk in. We parked, collected our gear, and walked the mile or so into "Rainbow land"—the space in the National Forest where people camp, cook, and serve and eat meals in outdoor kitchens that feed all attendees for free, and make music in drum circles that sometimes go all night. Within Rainbow land, the informal rules and culture of the Rainbow Family prevail. These include looking people in the eye; saying "Welcome home" to anyone who has clearly just arrived, or to anyone at all really; cooking in outdoor kitchens, where food is made and served by an often evolving group of volunteers and where cooks announce when food is ready so that anyone hungry can come to eat; calling everyone "brother" or "sister" or "mama" or "family" and talking to anyone at any time; and making all decisions in councils through peaceful consensus. Yet at a Rainbow Gathering, no one has a definitive say on what anyone else chooses to do. It was at this small regional Gathering that I became introduced—and inspired.

Rainbow Gatherings have been happening since 1972. In 1970, a music festival event called Vortex took place in Oregon.[1] After that, some "tribes" of folks participating in the political counterculture, including peace activists and veterans returning from the Vietnam War,[2] got together to organize an event that they thought would be the best of all countercultural ideas they'd come to know: part rock concert (without the pricey ticket or port-a-potty lines); part motorcycle rally (without the alcohol); part New Age spiritual church where spiritualities, religions, and traditions of all kinds would be welcomed and honored (without the dogma or discipline); part life in the trenches (without the war)—a nonviolent, noncommercial Gathering, a prayer for peace where money was not a useful form of currency (except for donations to the "Magic Hat" that provide for food and supplies at the Gathering).

Thus, the first "Rainbow Gathering of the Tribes" occurred, with thousands of invitations mailed out to hippies, activists, other countercultural folk, and politicians across the country. The invitation requested that people come to attend a noncommercial, nonviolent, spiritual event where all could gather to pray for peace on a mountaintop in Colorado. In a report titled "Peace and Religious Festival Begins in Colorado," the *New York Times* described the Rainbow Gathering in 1972 as "young people by the thousands" who were "quietly gathering . . . for what they termed 'a religious festival.' . . . They came to meditate in the forest, to chant prayers together, talk over things and play flutes and guitars and drums under the spruce and aspen trees."[3] This description is still largely fitting for Gatherings today. At a Gathering, love is the vibe and improvisational music the rhythm.

These annual events have taken place every summer thereafter, and the Rainbow Family of the Living Light celebrated their forty-first year of gathering with their National Rainbow Gathering of the Tribes in 2012. Since the very first Gathering, all the food, water, and sanitary and medical facilities have been freely provided to all attendees through the voluntary labor and participation of attendees. People from all walks of life are accepted and welcomed for a temporary repose in the woods, where kindness and consensus prevail and where people can express themselves in almost any conceivable way without formal sanction.[4]

Today, regional Rainbow Gatherings happen all over the country during the summer and throughout the year, with many different regions of the United States hosting local events. There's even a Gathering that takes place in Florida in the winter, so that the Rainbow Family always has a place to be. Some full-time "road dogs" spend their entire year traveling from Gathering to Gathering. Others who attend Rainbow Gatherings are contemporary versions of the American hobo, full-time travelers for whom mobility itself is a virtue,[5] who attend Gatherings in between temporary spells in various towns. Many others come from jobs, homes, and communities across the nation to attend. The National Gathering officially takes place July 1–7 every summer, although there are people gathered at the site for weeks before and after the week of the main event.

In the United States, Gatherings always take place on National Forest land, where camping is free for those willing to collect firewood, shit in the woods, and leave no trace. For the Rainbow Family, this is key: the belief that Americans have the right to use land that is public, that is legally theirs, in order to peacefully gather, providing an alternative vision to mainstream society (what they call Babylon) where conceptions and practices of private property dominate the geographical, political, and cultural landscape. At a Rainbow Gathering, in contrast to Babylon,[6] subsistence is freely provided to all through collective work and assistance, kindness is openly shared, and no one is governed but everyone has the potential to govern themselves.

Before my first National Gathering, which took place in the Upper Peninsula of Michigan in 2002, I hadn't spent any time in a National Forest. I assume that's true for a lot of Americans these days. Now a decade later, I've camped in many National Forests throughout the country and I know that there's a lot of variation among them. But Rainbow Gatherings require that certain resources be available, and even though the National Gathering is in a different place every year, all of the sites chosen for a Gathering have to have these requisite elements.

First, there must be a place to park hundreds of cars, often a dirt Forest Service road that travels through the woods or an open meadow along such a road. Forest Service regulations require that all four tires of a vehicle must be parked off the road, so the road must have wide enough shoulders and must itself be wide enough that people can park without blocking two-way traffic.

Second, there must be enough water, often from a spring or stream, and it must be clean enough to be drinkable—even for infants, children, and pregnant women—after boiling or filtering. Finally, there must be a meadow (called "main meadow," where "main circle" occurs) large enough to accommodate hundreds or even thousands of people. A dinner meal takes place in this main meadow every evening throughout the Gathering (for at least the week of July 1–7 and often beginning earlier, at the end of June, if kitchens are prepared to serve). The incredible celebration of July 4 that marks the climax of the Gathering also takes place in this space.

Space for parking, a source of clean water, and a large open meadow—although Rainbow Gatherings take place at different sites every year, and each site presents different resources and challenges, these three assets are essential for a Rainbow Gathering. When describing the process of selecting a site, Butterfly Bill writes, "We never expected to find all of these things just the way we wanted them, but looked for a place that satisfied a balance of all these needs."[7]

National Forest land is used by lots of people for lots of different reasons; but if it can ever be considered wilderness,[8] a Gathering turns it into a unique sort of metropolis. Trails become densely packed with people, thousands of feet crossing them each day. Meadows get trampled to make room for trade circles, yoga sessions, masses of tents, shared meals, and lots of smiling faces. Dozens of kitchen facilities of various shapes and styles are constructed throughout the woods, built much like I imagine the outposts of trench warfare were. Large fire pits are topped with metal grates for cooking, earthen ovens are constructed out of mud for baking, serving stations are made with tree branches lashed together and then attached to tree trunks to form make-shift countertops, and trench latrines ("shitters") are dug nearby each kitchen (but not too near).

At the National Gathering in the thick northern woods of Michigan's Upper Peninsula, I swatted mosquitoes constantly as I wandered the trails and visited kitchens with names like "Turtle Soup" and "Lovin Ovens" and "Montana Mud." In these kitchens, people were gathered around playing music, making food, conversing, and connecting with strangers. I also spent time at "procrastination stations" where people take a pause from walking the trail to share stories, cigarettes, or snacks. Numerous times every day, I got hugs from strangers, heard the words "loving you" accompanied by direct eye contact and a smile from people I had never met, and sometimes got asked for my pocket trash—one way to both meet a stranger and help keep the woods clean. I came to know and love this temporary world in which people live, act, and interact differently in this collective experience called a Rainbow Gathering.

Ten years later, I still have friends unfamiliar with this unique social world asking me questions like, "What's with that Rainbow Fest?" I tell them it takes place July 1–7, with July 4 being the climax of attendance and celebration, in a different National Forest every year.[9] It is definitively not a festival like Woodstock, Bonnaroo, or Burning Man because it is not a ticketed event. This is an important ideological distinction—it is a totally noncommercial event where anyone can come, everything is free, and nothing can be purchased with the currency of cash. At the first Rainbow Gatherings, people would highlight the special nature of these events by exclaiming, "This is not a Dead show!"[10] (a reference to The Grateful Dead, a band that many of the first Rainbow Gathering attendees had likely seen perform during one of their notorious live shows while "on tour"), differentiating this noncommercial, more spiritually charged space from other countercultural happenings. At the 2012 Rainbow Gathering, I heard the phrase, "This is not Bonnaroo!"

used similarly by younger folks expressing dissatisfaction with people using cell phones in Rainbow land.

It is, in many ways, still as it was originally intended—a free, open gathering of people where anyone is welcome to come and all necessary subsistence is provided freely to all through the efforts of all participants. For many (but not all, perhaps not ever and certainly not now), the Gathering is about being peaceful, acting peacefully, and praying for peace. For some, Rainbow Gatherings actively demonstrate the possibility of a nonhierarchical, freely participatory, and freely providing society where peace prevails over violence and freedom over domination or repression.

The material systems established to provide food, water, sanitation facilities, and medical care at a Gathering are based upon lessons learned by Vietnam War veterans who helped the hippies from the city construct outdoor kitchens, latrines, and systems of sanitation.[11] Rainbow Gatherings involve a wide array of alternative technological arrangements and forms of material organization. They take place in remote natural settings without electricity, running water, or flush toilets. Yet the basic services usually provided by the technological systems that bring these things to mainstream society—food to eat, water to drink, a place to relieve yourself, and often even a place to bathe—are provided freely to all those who attend.

To support life at a Rainbow Gathering, gatherers establish what is essentially an extremely sophisticated form of camping. Food is cooked over fires or in earthen ovens, water is collected and filtered from a natural source and transported by an elaborate system of PVC piping, constructed and dismantled by gatherers, to wherever water is needed, and bowels are relieved in deep trench latrines dug by the gatherers, often with very comfortable makeshift toilets constructed over them, which are covered when full. Volunteers stationed at the Center for Alternative Living Medicine (CALM), the Gathering's version of MASH, provide free medical care and basic treatments for dehydration, poison ivy, minor cuts, and the like.

These systems are instituted, organized, maintained, and dismantled based on the principles of anarchistic participation and a belief in leave-no-trace environmental practices. Everyone's basic needs (food, water, sanitation, and medical care) are provided for without commercial or monetary systems—kitchens rely on their own resources, donations (called "kick-downs" in Rainbow vocabulary), and supplies purchased with money donated to the Magic Hat, which is the only acceptable way to use currency at a Gathering. The establishment and maintenance of these temporary systems involve, indeed require, mass participation.

The cultural systems present at a Rainbow Gathering blend an eclectic mix of New Age, Native American, and Eastern spirituality, countercultural values, egalitarian organization, participatory engagement, and—perhaps above all else—freedom. The result is an annually reoccurring ritual in which many people experience *collective effervescence*: a heightened sense of collectivity, connectivity, and social togetherness. Some people come to pray; others come to party. The key is the freedom to come participate and experience this unique social world that exists without many of the boundaries and limitations that confine everyday life in mainstream America, including boundaries like access to sustenance and medical care as well as boundaries like social exclusion and isolation.

One of the ways that the Rainbow Family communicates is through "raps." Although the words vary ever so slightly, you can find these raps posted or printed on pamphlets at the information booth of every Gathering (often referred to as simply "Information") on signs and banners throughout a Gathering, on an unofficial informational Rainbow website,[12] and at other locations in cyberspace.[13] These help to communicate the values and practices of the Rainbow Family and their rituals. Rap 107 expresses "Gathering Consciousness":

> Please protect this beautiful land. Walk softly. Allow Plants and Animals to Be. Harmonize, Blend in. Use only down, dead wood. Cut no living trees. Preserve the meadows, camp in the woods. Everyone sharing makes a strong human tribe! Please protect the water sources by staying out of DELICATE spring areas. Observe and respect flagging in spring areas. Avoid camping, peeing, washing above spring areas. Keep ALL soap out of streams, springs, creek, and lake! Use a bucket to take your bath at least 100 feet away from all sources of water. To be certain drinking water is safe: boil or filter it! Use the shitters. Join in shitter digging. Dig community shitters at least 200 feet from surface water and kitchens. Protect our health! Cover your waste with lime or cold ash, wash hands after. Break the fly/illness connection: shit-flies-food-you! Seek nearest kitchen when lime, TP, or hand wash are running low. Camp together—Establish neighborhoods. Community fires only! Each fire needs a 5-gallon bucket with water and a shovel for FIRE PROTECTION. If you are the last to leave a fire, SAFETY FIRST—PUT IT OUT! Build only rock-lined hearths for fires to prevent soil damage and root fires. Think hearth! Where the Earth and Heart meet. "Tempt Not Lest Ye Be Lifted From"—Be responsible for your animals. Keep them fed, on a leash, and out of the kitchens and springs. Love them, Gatherings are hard on them. Separate garbage for recycling. Find nearest collection point. Compost in pits only. Use your own Bowl and

Spoon! Participate in all activities, councils, work crews, and workshops. You are the Gathering! R-E-S-P-E-C-T your sisters and brothers energies. Health problems? Contact CALM! Notice the balance: earth, sky, trees, water and people! Alcohol is discouraged, guns are inappropriate. Violence is contrary to the Spirit of the Gathering. Please take no photographs or videos of people without permission. Buying and selling endangers our legal right to be here. The Magic Hat is our bank. Donations to the Magic Hat fund our needs. Enjoy the Gathering with an open heart. You are fulfilling the vision. Join us for July 4 silent contemplation and prayer for peace. We love you.

Rap 701, about the leave-no-trace ethic of the Rainbow Family, reads,

Pack it in—Pack it out! Clean up begins the day you arrive! Bring in only what is necessary. There is no janitor here. You are the cleanup crew! In preparation for leaving: Pack up all your trash, separate trash for recycling, and bring to the appropriate areas. Take it away. Take it far away. Do not impact the small towns near the Gathering. Dismantle and disappear your encampment. Vanish all traces. Fire rocks scattered, ashes cold out and buried, pits filled in. Latrines and compost holes covered over. String and twine get removed from tree limbs. Hardened ground gets aerated with tools for future root growth and moisture catch. All litter is picked up. Help with recycling. Where everyone helps, the effort is easy. NATURALIZE! Scatter logs, branches, leaves, disappear trails and renew forest habitat. Water systems are removed, cleaned, and stored for next year. The final crew reseeds appropriate seed to renew vegetation and complete the process. Help when asked to help. Transport as many riders as possible out of the area to aid our travels. Treat local folks with great kindness. They have been kind to us. Drive safely and share this love wherever you go!

At the 2012 National Gathering, I saw an informal, somewhat satirical "test" posted at Information asking the following (see Figure 1.1):

The Rainbow Gathering is:

A. Big sex, drugs, rock n roll party.
B. Exploration of our national forests.
C. Religious group that travels to the cathedral of nature to pray for world peace July 4.
D. Experiment in cooperative nonhierarchical living that presents an alternative to capitalism.
E. Preparation for living in the wild so we'll be ready when society collapses.

F. A big dating game that facilitates hookups and children.

G. Some of all of the above.

The "right" answer is, of course, G.

While I was examining this sign, a man who was volunteering at Information introduced himself. A middle-aged man with a long ponytail wearing overalls, he told me he has been attending Gatherings since the late 1980s. Pointing to the test, he said,

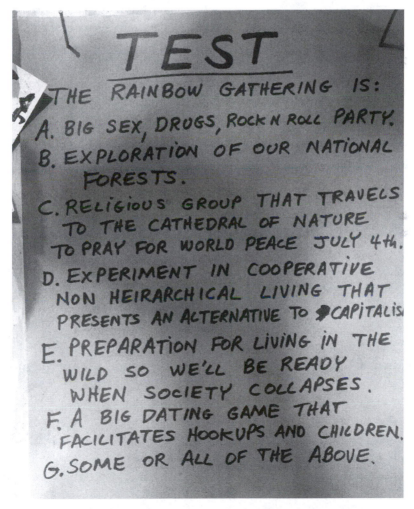

Figure 1.1: A Rainbow "test" posted at Information, 2012 National Gathering. *Source:* Chelsea Schelly.

Calling a Gathering any one of those things, or any one thing at all really, would be like calling a Swiss Army Knife a corkscrew. And the truth is, we don't do any one of those things particularly well. If you want a religious experience, join a church. If you want a dating game, join some online dating thing. If you want an experiment in living, join a commune. But the fact that we do a little bit of all of those things, that's really the amazing part in itself. We don't do any of it real well, but we are a space for all of it and so much more, and that it all comes together and we can actually pull it off, that's what's really incredible.

But what might you actually do at a Gathering? Well, talk to strangers, certainly. But they are no longer strangers when you arrive; they are Family. And with them, you can do almost anything. There are trade circles, where people barter for goods like clothing, candy bars, pretty rocks and gemstones, and illicit substances like marijuana or psychedelic mushrooms. Importantly, money is not an accepted form of currency. You do not pay for the necessities of food and water; even tobacco is free, as a group of folks who call themselves "Nic at Night" carry around tobacco products to distribute and yell things like, "You need a cigarette, I got a cigarette, you got a cigarette, I need a cigarette! Nic at Night!!!" at all times of the day and night.

There are drum circles, where people play drums together while others often dance, all night and sometimes all day too. Music is an important part of the Gathering, although it's never a ticketed event. You'll certainly hear different kinds of drums and various drumming rhythms, and you'll likely hear guitars, fiddles, singing, harmonicas, and even accordions spontaneously creating together. During the day, musicians wander the trails playing alone or gather randomly along the trails and around kitchens to play together. At night, music is a central component of the campfire circle, with both loud drumming and quieter musical interludes taking place at various "bliss pits" or "boogie pits" (campfires for hanging out around, rather than for cooking) scattered throughout the forest. There are also live theatrics nightly at the Granola Funk Theater; the theater crew constructs impressively massive and elaborate stages every year to host talent shows, open jam sessions, and other performances.

You might spend your days helping to carry food or water up and down the trail or helping to prepare meals; helpful participation is an integral part of Rainbow Family culture, sometimes even referred to as "the Rainbow way." You might also go for an organized botany walk, attend a yoga session, or listen to a lecture on spirituality at the Krishna Kitchen or Jesus Camp. There are classes and workshops on various topics from leather working and survival skills to yoga, psychic healing, and emotional support. You may wander the trails, sitting down to rest at procrastination stations or visiting various kitchens in response to calls of "Free food in the woods!"

An organized meal, "main circle" or "dinner circle," happens nightly in the main meadow. The sound of a conch shell and/or a mass of voices yelling "Circle!" indicates that it's time to start gathering for dinner. Once the food has arrived and a few quick daily announcements are made, people join hands in an "Om" circle[14] prior to being fed by the numerous kitchens that haul five-gallon pots or buckets to serve simple, delicious (and occasionally not-so-delicious) vegetarian food to all those present. The ending of the Om is admittedly always a little awkward, as no one individual decides when it's over; but when people start to raise their still connected hands into the air, the humming sound stops and a loud collective yelp of joy is released. Butterfly Bill, who has been attending Rainbow Gatherings for over two decades, describes dinner circle this way: "There was never anybody in the middle of the circle directing the others . . . each succeeding part of this ritual would arise spontaneously from someone out in the circle. After the cheer was over everyone sat down, except 'children and pregnant or nursing mothers,' who could come out to the center with their dishes and get served first."[15]

July 4 is the most organized day of the National Rainbow Gathering; people (mostly) spend the morning in silence. This silence is intended to provide a time for intentional prayer and reflection, but it is also an amazing demonstration of how thousands of people have come to connect in this unique social world. Through eye contact and hugs, people spend the morning speaking without words. Then, at "Rainbow noon" (when the sun is high in the sky; there are no clocks, or at least very few clocks, which are sometimes referred to as "Baby-lo-meters"), people gather in the main meadow and join hands, forming a huge circle, and Om. The circle is broken by a parade of children, and the afternoon is spent in raucous and joyous celebration. Often, plentiful slices of watermelon and other delicious treats (typically fruit, not candy or chocolate) are passed around. People drum and dance long into the night, and hugs and shouts of "we love you" abound.

Real-Life Experiences at Night:
One Evening at a National Rainbow Gathering[16]

Hearing the sounding of the conch shell, I make my way up the trail toward main meadow. It's dinnertime, and I'm hungry. As I enter the meadow, I see others already congregating—happy, smiling faces, some standing, some sitting, some gathered and chatting, others alone or quiet, some playing with their dogs, some hugging. Many other people are streaming into the meadow from the multiple trails that lead there. It's July 1, and this is going to be the biggest main meadow dinner thus far in the Gathering; main circle meals started a few days earlier this year. Volunteers from several different kitchens are carrying big, heavy pots into the meadow, some hauling them there with wagons, others using tree limbs stretched between two sets of shoulders. Some kitchen crews are already gathered in the center of the meadow, getting ready to serve. A circle is forming organically, as people move back toward the edges of the meadow to let newcomers join in.

The conch shell sounds three more times while I sit and watch and wait contentedly. Then, a slender older man with a long grey ponytail silences the crowd with a loud "Ho!" and makes a few announcements. He announces, as he does every night and as he will continue to do at every communal dinner throughout the Gathering, that the Forest Service could ticket or tow any car that doesn't have all four tires off the road. He tells the crowd to stay healthy by making sure that all water is boiled or filtered before drinking and reminds the kitchens that they need to boil or filter all the water they serve. He reminds everyone to use the community shitters, to cover their shit with ash or lime, and to wash their hands. After he's finished speaking, without any need for notification, the crowd begins to stand and join hands. The kitchen volunteers create their own small circle in the center, surrounded by all those who have gathered to eat. Then the Om begins, as everyone in the circle lets out the sacred sound and connects with the other breaths around them, like a nightly rehearsal for the big day.

As the children and pregnant women make their way to the center to be served after the Om circle has ended, the rest of us in the circle sit and wait to be served. Kitchen volunteers carry their pots around the circle offering food. I follow the accepted standards of food serving, intended to keep things sanitary: I hold my bowl beside and below the rim of their big serving pots, and they ladle food into my bowl without touching it. Each serving pot starts at a different point in the circle and goes around until it is empty or everyone is content, whichever happens first. This evening, a large shirtless man in denim overalls is walking around the circle yelling "Yeast!"—nutritional yeast is a beneficial and delicious additive to any Rainbow meal. The "yeast man" makes me smile, as I have heard that same yell at many of the main circle meals at the several National Gatherings I've attended in the past decade.

A few minutes after the yeast man has made his final round, the "Magic Hat" crew begins. A group of half a dozen musicians parade around the circle singing impromptu tunes like "The Magic Hat, it keeps us fat; we share our food, and sharing is good." One person in the group carries a five-gallon bucket with "Magic Hat" written in marker on the side and collects monetary donations, which go to Main Supply for purchasing food for the Gathering.

While munching on rice and beans, sautéed vegetables, and potato soup,[17] I think to myself, that's one of the great things about Rainbow: People figure out what they can do, and what they enjoy doing, and they are able to do it. Whether it's bringing and sharing yeast, digging really good latrines, policing the traffic in the parking lot by yelling "Slow down!" and "Six up!" and "Welcome home!" all day and night, leading yoga classes, or cooking delicious food out of simple ingredients for hundreds of people in the woods, all sorts of people with different personalities, interests, and talents can pitch in here and create a whole world through their voluntary efforts.

After dinner, my dogs lick my bowl clean and I make a mental note to clean it at the next kitchen bus station I see. The series of bleach water rinses, usually organized into three five-gallon buckets of varying levels of soap, water, and bleach, is certainly cleaner than a dog's mouth, although many bowls at Rainbow are first licked clean by a canine. There are a lot of dogs here, and other animals—I've seen cats, birds, ferrets, a pet rat, a pet snake, a pet rooster, and even a potbellied pig at the Gatherings I've attended.

I stand and look up at the sky. It is almost nightfall. Some would say that the nights at a Gathering are the best part of it all; as Emile Durkheim once noted, "The very act of congregating is an exceptionally powerful stimulant. . . . If it is added that the ceremonies are generally held at night, in the midst of shadow pierced here and there by firelight, we can easily imagine the effect that scenes like these are bound to have on the minds of all those who take part."[18]

Walking up the trail, I am stopped by a group of men sitting along the road yelling, "Joke, toke, or smoke!" This type of roadblock is typical here, and these men are requesting a joke, some marijuana, or a cigarette from everyone who walks by. Just another way to have fun interacting with strangers, I think to myself. I tell them I don't really know any jokes, and they tell me, "Then you gotta drink some watta!" They have modified the "joke, toke, or smoke" roadblock idea by offering water to everyone who tries to walk by without a contribution.

"What a great modification!" I tell them as I drink from their communal jug, careful not to touch my lips to it, another common Rainbow courtesy related to sanitation. "Great idea for keeping people hydrated," I say. "Thank you!" As I continue wandering down the trail, I yell back at them, "Lovin' you, brothers!"

I stop to sit down at the first campfire I see, which is—as they usually are—located near a kitchen. This is Jesus Kitchen, organized by a group of Christians, a regular kitchen at every National Gathering. Here, no one smokes or swears and the energy is serene and calming. There's a guitar and drum duo playing music, and I sit close to listen. Then darkness surrounds us. The duo keep playing, the light of the campfire flickering across their hands and faces as they play. After a while, I find my flashlight buried in my bag and walk on. Along the trail, smiling faces have turned into sounds and shadows; the soft reverberations of footsteps and laughter and chatting anonymously pass by me. As I'm wandering slowly down main trail, someone stops me to say, "There's a kitchen this direction called Katuah, and they're having a big party tonight, a huge drum circle, and lots of yummy treats. Follow me!" And I do, reversing direction to walk with this voice in the shadows, a woman who introduces herself as Calico as she continues making her announcement to all those we pass.

A large fire in a heart-shaped boogie pit is already gleaming, and people are sitting on makeshift log benches and on the ground around it. Some drumming has started, but it's still relatively quiet. People are busy working by lantern light in the kitchen, baking in the earthen ovens they worked so hard to build, but will willingly destroy a week (or two or three) from now when they leave. Soon they are serving cookies (made with marijuana oil). As those around the circle munch on cookies and compliment the cooks, we hear a booming call of "We love you!" coming from a multitude of voices far off in the woods. After the long, drawn out chant is over (it usually ends up sounding something like "Weeeeeeeeeee Loooooooovvvvvvve Yoooooooouuuuuu!"), a loud male nearby immediately shouts, "On the count of three!" Cued by the countdown, the large group congregated around the fire yells "We love you!" simultaneously in reply. We hear several other groups responding, the shouts bouncing off the trees and echoing through the woods, before the calls are overtaken by the beat of the drums.

Then the drummers really get going, and all the sounds of night are drowned out by the thumping rhythms. It is hard to tell how many people are drumming or watching, because I stay seated very near the fire as I feel the crowd behind me swell and then slowly begin to wane. It is enchanting—the flicker of the fire casting brilliant light and shadow on the drummers' hands and faces, the pulsation of the deep rhythms, the sounds of joy as people congregated around sitting, standing, or dancing let out spontaneous shouts and yips and yells of glee.

Deciding it's time to head back to my tent, I slowly stand. I wait until I am back on the trail, away from the folks still gathered around the fire and the few drummers still playing, before turning on my flashlight, cognizant of Rainbow Family courtesy surrounding flashlights and the respectful ways to avoid blinding others with the artificial light. As I navigate the darkness, voices continue to pass me. There are spontaneous and random yells of "Yeah!" and "Yee-haw!" and others noises of joy coming from all directions as I walk. Before I've made it to my tent, another round of "We love you!" echoes through the woods. Since I'm alone, I shout it out with every one.

Crafting Collectivity at a Rainbow Gathering

So what's with that Rainbow Fest, really? First of all, as I've already mentioned, it's not a festival like Burning Man or Bonnaroo. Rainbow Gatherings are free, noncommercial events open to all who choose to attend. Further, people who come to a Rainbow Gathering share more than simply a love of a particular band, style of music, or even form of artistic expression. They share in the experiences of an entire social world with its own unique forms of material and social organization, cultural norms and rituals guiding action and interaction, and even language and forms of expression.

Although Forest Service regulations technically require group camping permits for large groups—and Rainbow Gatherings draw a very, very large group, with thousands of people attending every National Gathering—the Rainbow Family officially refuses to sign them, arguing that no one can represent or speak on behalf of the group. When on trial for failing to obtain a group camping permit for the 2000 National Gathering, Plunker (a "Rainbow name"), who has identified as a member of the Rainbow Family for decades, wrote that the Rainbow Family is "not a 'who' or a 'what,' but a 'Tao' or 'Way,' or Creed. 'Rainbow Family' is a spiritual ideal, and no one can legally file in court for 'Rainbow Family' anymore than they can legally file in court on behalf of 'Jesus Christ.'"[19]

Perhaps most well known for his studies on religion, sociologist Emile Durkheim once wrote, "A society whose members are united by the fact that they represent the sacred world and its relations with the profane world in the same way, and by the fact that they translate these common ideas into common practice, is what we call a church."[20] Based on this definition, the Rainbow Family represents a church for many—but certainly not all—of those who gather, pointing to one of the major tensions in Rainbow culture. Some people who gather even refer to the Gathering as a church—they use this language in conversation and in phrases like "Keep the alcohol out of the church!" and "No guns in the church!" (I've heard this second phrase used in reference to both violent behavior and the presence of law enforcement).

"Rainbow land" (the space in the National Forest where a Gathering is taking place) is, in the language of Emile Durkheim, a sacred space comprised of sacred ritual action and interaction as well as sacred objects and sacred language. It is important to most gatherers that this space is a natural environment classified as public land; in the Rainbow Family, the natural world is considered sacred, and many of the practices that gatherers engage in while at a Gathering are themselves seen as sacred. Hugs and smiles are sacred forms of communication in Rainbow land. Your own dish and silverware, called "bliss ware" and carried with you at all times while in Rainbow land so that you can eat anytime a kitchen is serving, are sacred objects. Rainbow land stands in marked contrast to "Babylon," the entire world outside the Rainbow Gathering, which is considered profane. Although the word *profane* sometimes implies something dirty or corrupted, Durkheim used it to mean something banal, ordinary, and decidedly outside the sacred world.[21]

National Rainbow Gatherings are rituals that temporarily heighten feelings of connectivity, creating a sense of what Emile Durkheim called *collective effervescence*.[22] Durkheim told us long ago that society is more than a collection of individuals, more than the sum of its parts. People sense that when they experience moments of collective effervescence, when they can feel themselves connecting to something beyond themselves and they allow this feeling to shape their thoughts and actions. Durkheim used the term *collective effervescence* to "capture the idea of social force at its birth."[23] For Durkheim, collective effervescence is the experience of profound connection to society and the social energy that exists both because of and outside of ourselves. Collective effervescence describes moments or extended periods in which we can feel the collective energy of something greater than—yet dwelling within—ourselves, when we feel energetically and emotionally connected to a sense of the whole that shapes our ideas and actions.[24]

Describing such moments of heightened connectivity, Marcel Mauss tells us that the experience "is pre-eminently collective. By this, we do not simply mean that festivities are celebrated in common, but that the feeling which the community has of itself and its unity suffuses all its actions. Festivities are not only collective in the sense that very many individuals assemble to take part; they are the object and expression of the group."[25] The power of collective effervescence "is such that it allows individuals to be incorporated into a collectivity by substituting the world immediately available to their perceptions for another, moral world in which people can interact on the basis of shared understandings."[26] At a Rainbow Gathering, a unique social world based on particular yet shared understandings is crafted through interactional processes that shape both material and cultural organization; the interaction rituals of a Rainbow Gathering help to craft a profound sense of social connectivity.

Rainbow Gatherings also have characteristics similar to anthropologist Victor Turner's discussion of "communitas"—"an essential and generic human bond"[27] involving relations with a spontaneous nature that are "more than classifications, since they incite men to action as well as to thought."[28] *Communitas* is "a transformative experience that goes to the heart of each person's being and finds in it something profoundly communal and shared."[29]

At the National Rainbow Gathering, individuals come together and experience ways of being, doing, and feeling that reinforce and amplify a collective spirit and sense of connection as people feel the energy of the social and their oneness with it. Many people experience a heightened sense of collective effervescence, and the material structures, cultural systems, and interaction rituals[30] of a Gathering contribute to and foster the development of this collective connectivity. As we'll see in the pages that follow, everything about Rainbow Gatherings—their physical structure, their material systems, their means of organization, and their unique forms of communication and interaction—works to contribute to the feelings of collectivity temporarily experienced by many of those who participate in this annually reoccurring ritual.

Durkheim thought that all religions shared a root source: to help people make sense of a feeling of collectivity and connection to the social group that they do not yet recognize as the collective power of society itself. Durkheim thought that the "religious nature of man" is "an essential and permanent aspect of humanity."[31] For most participants, the Gathering is a ritual with spiritual purpose and the emotional high of collective effervescence does take on a religious or spiritual expression.

In some ways, Gatherings are like Sunday church services—they are temporary, reoccurring ritual events that foster a sense of collective effervescence. However, Rainbow Gatherings happen annually rather than weekly and in an ever-changing natural environment rather than in a designated building. Further, the ritual is not even ostensibly about connecting to a particular deity but rather about connecting human beings to one another and demonstrating the viability of peaceful freedom among participants through both intention and practice. The ritual itself is geared toward bringing about a heightened awareness of connectivity through participation and through the struggles inherent in actually practicing freedom and acceptance, nonhierarchical decision making, and noncoercive cultural forms.

The experience of a Rainbow Gathering is different for everyone and has different meanings for different people. Some people come and don't really recognize or participate in the ritual. Some people sit alone in their tent all day; some people hang out in the parking lot drinking beer. Rainbow Gatherings are incredibly anarchistic—no leaders, no enforcers, no requirements or sanctions. All sorts of people come and do all sorts of things, some of which certainly contradict the peacefulness of the party. Not everyone experiences, or seeks to experience, the collective spiritual and emotional high that many gatherers feel at Gatherings.

Yet the overall effect is a reoccurring heightening of the collective spirit among those who identify with it and participate in it. It happens every year, again and again, different but the same. Rainbow Gatherings have been incredibly successful in creating this sense of collective effervescence, of crafting a collective energy and sense of connection, for four decades. Several generations of Rainbow Family have now experienced the heightened social energy and sense of social connectivity that occur at this annual ritual, as founders (hippies, Vietnam veterans, and back-to-the-landers who were themselves young in 1972) have become elders, and their children have become adults and themselves parents of children who identify with the Rainbow Family.

The people who come to Rainbow Gatherings to actively participate in the voluntary labor, shared resources, loving culture, and communal experience feel a sense of collective effervescence generated by their very participation in the ritual. All of the processes of organizing material systems and the structures of decision making as well as the cultural expressions and interactional norms of a Gathering contribute to this energy that connects individuals to a social collective. Perhaps most interesting, even the contradictions within the Family—the presence of violent behavior at a prayer for peace, the presence of people who speak and act in ways that actively conflict with the peaceful and loving vibe of the Gathering—can actually increase the experience of collective effervescence within this social world for those who experience it. Even contradictions (or more specifically the acceptance of contradictory people) actually, tenuously, work to heighten the sense of collective effervescence experienced at a Gathering.

This is because the most important value of the Rainbow Family, arguably, is freedom—the freedom to be and do as you choose. Rainbow Gatherings are anarchistic in many ways, but they are not complete chaos. Most people participate in a shared culture of norms, values, and practices, at least to some extent. Most people are incredibly empowered by the ability to freely participate in any way they choose and by being rewarded immediately for their efforts through other people's positivity and appreciation. Most people experience the sense of collective effervescence, the crafted connectivity, which develops among thousands of people temporarily gathered every summer in a National Forest.

Not everyone who attends a Gathering experiences a heightened sense of sacred social togetherness. Not everyone helps out, not everyone practices peace or respect or nonviolence, and not everyone experiences the collective high that the Rainbow Gathering ritual can provide. Yet everyone is welcome at a Gathering, and people can act and do and say as they please with very few restrictions or sanctions on behavior. This freedom is complicated, as there are certainly people in the Family who wish that everyone would do, act, and be exactly as they themselves are. It is qualified, as people are responsible for their own actions (especially with regard to respecting the natural environment, as we will see in Chapter 7) and are expected not to hinder the freedom of others. The social world of a Rainbow Gathering is in many ways a ritual of freedom, an experiment in living coming closer to resembling true liberty[32]—with all of the potential and confusion that it brings—than any other social world I've known.

Chapter 2
Who Goes Home?

The first Rainbow Gathering participants I met outside of my friends who introduced me to the events and took me "home" were the four men who ran the main kitchen at my first Gathering, the small Oklahoma regional Gathering in 2002. I don't remember their Rainbow names[1] anymore, but I still remember them well—four middle-aged men, one balding and with a potbelly, one with long hair and a very large grey beard, all dressed colorfully, sometimes wearing long skirts. People rarely talk about their Babylonian lives at a Rainbow Gathering, but I heard two of them say things—about kids these days and summers off— that indicated they were schoolteachers. In between hugs exchanged frequently and freely between one another and anyone and everyone else who wanted one, they made sure the water dispenser was full, built fires (one for cooking, one for gathering around), made coffee and their version of doughnuts (fried dough covered in powdered sugar) in the morning, prepared snacks all day, cooked dinner, and yelled out for volunteers to come help with whatever needed done.

One morning, three Forest Service rangers approached the kitchen while I was sitting around an early fire sipping campfire coffee (made by simply boiling a big pot of water with coffee grounds in it) with a small handful of sleepy folks. We knew that the rangers were coming because campers further down the trail were yelling "Six up!"—the Rainbow term indicating the presence of law enforcement, a call that follows them everywhere they go at every Rainbow Gathering—long before the officers were in sight of the kitchen.

The man with the big beard, an experienced gatherer and thus used to interacting with Forest Service rangers, immediately said good morning and offered the rangers coffee and a doughnut. Although they declined, they seemed to appreciate the offer.[2]

"Good morning to you," one of the two male rangers said. "We were wondering if you could tell us how many people have come to camp with you here today?" The rangers of course know that this is a Gathering of the Oklahoma Rainbow Tribe, a group opposed to signing any permits or registering any camp as part of their belief that none of them can sign or speak for any other, and that public land—as long as it's used responsibly—should be freely available for public use. The bearded man, of course, also knows all this.

"Oh, I'd say about 71," he replied with a wide, cheeky grin; or maybe it was 70, or 72. I don't remember the exact number, although I know it was under 75. He explained to the group a moment later, after the rangers had walked away, that the important thing was that he'd given a number just shy of that at which the Forest Service requires a group camping permit.[3] In reality, there were probably close to 150 people at that small regional Gathering.

The rangers laughed, said okay, and walked away. As they departed, the man shouted, "Sure you don't want a doughnut? Free food in the woods! Lovin' you!" We could hear them chuckling as they walked off down the trail. Friendly, articulate, eccentric, and aware—this describes the bearded man and many of the other Rainbow Gathering participants I've met.

Describing the Rainbow Family of the Living Light[4]

The Rainbow Family of the Living Light is an incredibly diverse family. Walking down any Rainbow trail, you are likely to see people of every age, from infants to elders. Based on my own observations at Gatherings, I'd say the most highly represented age demographics are the aging hippies of the 1960s and 1970s, still dressed in tie-dye and flowing fabrics and sometimes leather, and the younger generation of teens and young adults, who don more piercings and tattoos and avoid most of the colorful clothing of the older generations.[5]

Don't let this characterization downplay the really amazing diversity of the Rainbow Family; you can meet people from many different regions, eras, and walks of life at a Gathering. There are Christians, Krishna devotees, and Jewish folks; young people and old; people of all races and ethnicities and even people from different countries; and people with all kinds of abilities and disabilities. I've met people in wheelchairs and a man with one leg at Gatherings, and most of the "isms" and prejudices that exist in Babylon simply do not hold the same weight in Rainbow land, where people of all ages, colors, shapes, and sizes are greeted without outward or systemic stereotyping or prejudice.[6]

At a Rainbow Gathering, "what" you are and where you come from matter a whole lot less than what you do while you're there, how you treat other people, and what you contribute to the energy of the event through your participation. As Butterfly Bill puts it, at a Rainbow Gathering,

> nobody cared about what you were before on the outside. It didn't matter if you were rich or poor, young or old, educated or not. . . . Very basic traits of moral character came out in people if they had them in themselves, and they were recognized and appreciated when they did—traits like honesty, industriousness, perseverance, prudence, compassion, understanding, helpfulness, and unselfishness. . . . Less desirable traits also came out if given the unchastised [*sic*] freedom to. . . . It was a most basic test of a person to observe what he or she did upon the blank slate of the gathering, and as such it was the best self-discovery seminar that had ever been devised.[7]

Attendance at the annual National Rainbow Gathering is massive, with literally thousands of people coming to gather. I've heard estimates ranging from 5,000 to 50,000 at the National Gatherings I've been to.[8] Personally, I'm liable to believe the lower approximations, although any estimate is bound to be inaccurate. Rainbow Gatherings involve a population that is really difficult to count because people can camp anywhere, be anywhere at any time, and not everyone attends any one event, even the main circle that takes place in main meadow on July 4. Just like the earliest years of Rainbow Gatherings, many of the people you meet are veterans of war, although forty years later, the United States has unfortunately been involved in several other wars from which they have come home.

Some people at Gatherings, particularly those who show up early to help set up and stay late to help clean up, are full-time travelers, modern hobos, nomads who wander the country hitchhiking or train hopping, in shared cars or buses, or on foot, following Gatherings, other festivals, temporary work opportunities, or wanderlust.[9] Many other people are full-time professionals who take a few days of vacation time to come spend the Fourth of July at the

Gathering. A longtime Rainbow Family participant who calls himself Tigger estimates that about 85 percent of people who attend Gatherings "live inside; they live in regular homes."[10]

Yet you rarely hear people talking about the specifics of their life in Babylon at a Gathering. People connect over places they've been, common people they know, musical interests, knowledge of nature and farming, or general life experiences like marriage, divorce, birth, and death but seldom over educational attainment, careers, or salaries. Thus, it is difficult to classify the Rainbow Family based on standard sociological or demographic categories, but this aspect of Rainbow culture is an important part of the open and egalitarian experience and the ritual of community shared by many of those who gather.

Rolling Stones writer Tim Cahill divided the attendees of the first National Gathering in 1972 "into a quartet of categories: 1) those who came for a rock festival, 2) those who came to be with people like themselves, and simply draw strength from congregation, 3) lost souls and acid crawlbacks, seeking structure in life, or a cosmic message, 4) the fishers of souls, believers and gurus, looking for recruits, or more exactly, converts."[11]

At the 2012 National Gathering, an elder who calls himself Preacher told me, "It used to be just the hippies, tramps, weekend warriors, and the yogis. But now it's a whole lot more diverse than that. That's good, but it brings its own issues because the messages seem to get a little muddled."

Today, peaceful, loving hippie types of all ages continue to attend Gatherings, attempting to foster a community of hopefulness and peace through their participation in the Rainbow Family. Regardless of their outside professions, interests, ages, or income categories, these folks can connect over compassion-based eating practices, communication styles, and parenting choices as well as The Grateful Dead and Buddhism. Young college kids looking for a good party also come to Gatherings. Successful doctors and lawyers who still feel connected with the values and hopes of the hippie counterculture attend, and so do homeless alcoholics and wounded veterans. There are dispossessed, angry, and sometimes even violent individuals of all ages who find a home in Rainbow like no other they've known, accepting of even their most unsocial habits and graces. It is my experience that more of the young travelers today, like my friends Patches, Turtle, Skittles, and Squirrel, are less like the older generation of Rainbow hippies in their fashion sense, communication style, and ways of acting. They tend more toward dark-colored clothing, drink more alcohol, and in general seem more dispossessed; not interested in or able to see their capacity to change mainstream society or the things they don't like about the world, they instead seem to be turning away from it.

Perhaps it is easier to describe the variety of folks in the Rainbow Family through categorizations. These categories are certainly not mutually exclusive: some people fit in multiple categories. They aren't likely exhaustive either; there are many people I haven't met who have been to Gatherings or identify with the Rainbow Family. Yet they may help someone unfamiliar with this unique social world understand at least some of the diversity in experience, position, and worldview among the attendees of a Rainbow Gathering.

Older Folks and the Elders

At any National Rainbow Gathering, you are likely to meet someone who has been to twenty or more of these annual events. It's not difficult to find someone who claims they were there at the very beginning; these older folks are an integral part of making this social world what it is. Given the limits of age and health, many are unable to run kitchens or do much of the hard physical work required at a Gathering anymore. Yet given the benefits of age and experience, the older folks at the Gathering are respected for their wisdom. Respect for this first generation of Rainbow Family (who are often veterans of the Vietnam War, Grateful Dead tours, or both) is a part of Rainbow culture. Some claim to be shamans or medicine men, and some tell stories of Rainbow history (sometimes referred to as "hipstory" by gatherers) or the counterculture of the 1960s. Together they help to keep the past alive. Many still come in tie-dye and many continue to live the political radicalism of the 1960s, still concerned about our constitutional right to publicly gather, police harassment, political conspiracy, and the power of peace.

The elders are a subset of the older, experienced Family members who actively participate in the non-organized organization of Rainbow Gatherings. Elders help to run CALM (the Center for Alternative Living Medicine, the entirely volunteer medical service providers of the Gathering), participate in various councils (the completely open meetings in which decisions are made by consensus), and serve as facilitators in myriad other ways. Teddy, a shirtless man with long, thick curls and a big smile, is younger than the elders, although he helps coordinate the main circle meal and has been actively involved in organization and facilitation at the past four National Gatherings. He told me that "it's really hard to say how many [elders] there are, because everyone involved would count them differently;

who's included wouldn't be the same for everyone." Yet identifying someone as an elder at a Gathering is an indication of respect and position; although there is no formal hierarchy at Rainbow, older folks are often given respect based on age and experience, contrary to what they might encounter in mainstream society, where ageism as well as class-based judgments often negatively impact the interactional experiences of those with wrinkles and wisdom.

There are also older folks who end up at a Rainbow Gathering for the first time at this later stage in their life. In my experience, coming to Rainbow is often associated with running away from something or starting a new chapter in life. I've met older folks hiding from the law (shirking drug use convictions or unpaid medical bills; I've never met someone avoiding punishment for a violent crime). I've met older addicts looking for a place to clean up. I've met older folks who've hit rock bottom due to divorce, job loss, or death of a loved one who come because—like me at seventeen—they were looking for something different, learned about Rainbow through a casual conversation with a stranger or a new acquaintance, and came hoping to experience something more positive and meaningful (or perhaps just less negative and devastating) than what their profane lives in Babylon had to offer.

Younger Folks, Runaways, and Children of the State

There are a lot of younger folks (late teens to early thirties) at Gatherings. Some of them come with their parents who were 1960s generation hippies; others come during their summer break from college. Some college students and college-age folks come because they heard about Rainbow Gatherings through MTV or the marijuana-themed magazine High Times, who have both reported on Rainbow Gatherings as one of the best parties of the year. Some young folks come just looking to party, bringing their own drugs or finding them when they arrive, staying up all night and simply having a good time like they would at a music festival or other summer vacation with friends.

The younger folks who do get involved in the organization of a Gathering do a lot of the hard, physical work—pushing and pulling carts of kitchen supplies up the trails, digging deep trenches for shitters, building fire pits and earthen ovens, and carrying water to kitchens. Many of the younger folks who come to Rainbow Gatherings are street kids in a general sense, runaways or kids without the support systems that come with childhood for many Americans. Among participants who completed a health survey done at the 2005 National Gathering in West Virginia, almost 30 percent had been forced to leave or had run away from home before reaching the age of eighteen.[12] In 2012, I asked an elder who called herself Sharing about the presence of street kids, young full-time travelers, at Gatherings. She told me, "There are certainly more of them than there used to be. One reason is there just aren't as many free places to crash. A lot of the free culture of the sixties is gone elsewhere, but it's still alive here." She added, "And what on earth do they have to look forward to? I can't imagine being a young person nowadays."

I met Patches, Turtle, Skittles, and Squirrel at my first National Rainbow Gathering, in the Upper Peninsula of Michigan, in 2002. All four were my age at the time—around eighteen—but all four had been "traveling"—running away from foster homes, hitchhiking, hopping trains, and staying in shelters—for years: Turtle and Squirrel for four, Patches for three, Skittles for two. All four were what I've heard other gatherers call "state department kids"—runaways from broken families and foster homes who made a life for themselves on the road rather than stay and deal with the hand life dealt them in Babylon.

While driving across Nebraska in the spring of 2012, my partner Dave and I picked up a young couple hitchhiking. Both eighteen years old, they had met as street kids in Boulder, Colorado, and were heading toward the National Rainbow Gathering. "I've never been," the young man told us, "but we've both heard that we'll be welcome there, and I'm ready for a break from sleeping on the streets. It's probably more comfortable sleeping in the woods, if you're homeless." These two also said they'd been traveling for years; her for four, him for two. These kids are characteristic examples of the lost and broken young men and women who sometimes come to Rainbow. Unlike most men and women in America, they have no backup plan—no parents to ask for help, no place to fall back on for support in times of need. Often, they find some temporary support and sense of belongingness in the Rainbow Family.

I met Sherlock at the 2012 Gathering in Tennessee. Traveling on a school bus with dozens of other young folks, he was helping to run a kitchen called Fat Kids[13] at the Gathering. While I was sitting on the main trail, taking a rest from carrying a heavy load into camp, he politely asked, "Do you mind if I join you to rest?" We introduced ourselves and started chatting. He asked me how long I've been traveling (a much more typical way to start a conversation at a Gathering than asking the standard "What do you do?" question that actually means, much more narrowly, how do you make money). I, in turn, asked him the same.

"Eight years," he told me. "I finished high school a year early, and I wasn't really liking what society had to offer. I wanted to go see if I could find a way to be free."

I asked him, "Is this it?"

He responded with a certain "Yes." After a pause he added, "Well, I'm not complaining."

Children

You might assume that a Rainbow Gathering is not an ideal place for children, given the prevalence of illicit drugs, big dogs, and the difficulties of outdoor life that range from snakes and ticks to the necessities of water filtration and sanitation. Yet there are many children, from newborns to teenagers, who come to Gatherings with their parent or parents, and life at a Gathering is different than life elsewhere for children just as much as for adults.

There is a camp at every National Rainbow Gathering called Kid Village (or Kiddie Village or Kiddy Village) so that families with children can always find one another and camp together if they choose to (although not everyone with kids camps here). Kid Village is vehemently anti-alcohol and kid friendly, where people—including those who aren't parents—are expected to interact with and help care for children in peaceful, loving, and child-centered ways. Kid Village has its own kitchen, the only kitchen that receives food from Main Supply even though it does not serve the main dinner circle, an indication of the Rainbow Family value of collectively providing for the littlest Family members.

In Kid Village and throughout the Gathering, care for children is often a much more collective act than in Babylon. I've seen kids walking around with adults who are not their parents carrying plastic bags and yelling "Pocket trash!"—a fun game to play with their current babysitter (although I've never heard anyone in Rainbow use that word). This type of collective care helps to provide a respite for parents who also want to participate in the Gathering in other ways.

Kids are also active participants in the Gathering experience. The young ones sometimes walk around naked, get their faces painted, and dance to the rhythm of a drum circle, sometimes just like mom or dad. Many post-toddler-age children learn to walk around the Gathering alone, asking for water and food from kitchens as they need it. Children learn the language of the Gathering; throughout the years, I've heard "Welcome home!" and "We love you!" (and even "Six up!") from many smiling children. Children are an integral part of the July 4 celebrations; a children's parade comes to the center of the circle at high noon, breaking the silence and indicating the commencement of the celebratory festivities.

Some children get intensely involved in the barter system of the Gathering, called trade circle, where people sit on blankets with their organized "tradeables" (a term for the trade goods such as rocks, knives, "zu zus" like candy bars and soda, clothes, art, drugs, camping supplies, and many other useful and desirable things) as in a free-for-all participatory flea market. You'll likely see at least a few kids swarming from blanket to blanket around the trade circle at any National Gathering, working the trade.

Some gatherers express dismay about the young children who turn into such calculated brokers in what is intended to be a noncommercial space.[14] Here, it is only important to note the participation of children in trade circle, which is for some a fundamental part of the Gathering experience. In all sorts of ways, children actively participate in the activities and energies, the interactions and culture, of the Rainbow Family. They meet other children and many other adults who greet them with love and positivity. And, like the parents who bring them, they too are energized and in turn actively participate in the energizing of the Gathering experience.

The Hippies

The hippie counterculture of the 1960s still lives on at a Rainbow Gathering, not as a throwback to an earlier era but rather through real styles, ideas, and ways of life that continue to provide meaning for individual lives. Many people who identify with the Rainbow Family also identify as hippies. The values of the hippie era—political activism, nonviolence, peacefulness, unbounded love, and mystical spirituality, among others—are still important to them. For some, this is the most important thing about Gatherings: they demonstrate the potential of the 1960s vision and the possibility of a world in which people treat each other with kindness and respect, where people's needs are met with compassion and equality, where egalitarianism and community prevail, and where humans live in environmentally and spiritually conscious ways.

Many people who identify with the Rainbow Family are politically active in their Babylonian lives in ways that match the values of the hippie counterculture. At the 2012 National Gathering, I saw several signs for the Occupy movement in the parking lot (anything more political than a conversation is usually kept outside of Rainbow land), including "Occupy the National Forest" written in the dust on a van window and another car with a "We are the 99%" sign propped up on its roof; one man brought a big, professionally made banner that said "Corporations Are Not People" to hang across his vehicle and stopped me in the parking lot to talk politics. Another participant described Gatherings "as a melding of politics and spirituality, 'as they go hand in hand, and in society people separate them.'"[15]

Spirituality at a Rainbow Gathering is important but not restrictive, arguably similar to what appealed to many of the hippies of an earlier era. Rainbow land is called a church, Krishna devotees and Christians both have big kitchens, Native American spirituality is deeply respected by many (even if it's not well understood), and talk of the universal spirit and oneness are common. The spiritual, mystical, and religious influences on the Rainbow Family are incredibly diverse, and the "mix is so rich and continuously in flux that any description of the Rainbow Family's roots must be inadequate."[16]

No matter what the belief system or spiritual orientation, religion and spirituality are deeply respected—and openly discussed—by many at Gatherings. I've talked with self-described "homeless bums" about God and Jesus. One of them told me, "You've got to believe in God, if you've lived my life. You just gotta." I've talked with a man about his serious faith in the Mayan prophecies and heard another talk very deeply about humans as simultaneously being sovereign individuals and spiritually connected entities. I've heard people talking about the sacredness of plants, of birth, and of death. In modern American society, where the only religions on the rise are arguably dogmatic and limited, the non-dogmatic spiritual salad bowl of the Rainbow Family is quite refreshing. For some, this spiritual energy centers the vision and opens the heart to the entire Rainbow Gathering experience.

The music of the 1960s counterculture still holds meaning for many who attend Gatherings: references to the Grateful Dead or Jerry (Garcia) are common, musicians play and sing songs of that era and culture, and even the most prevalent musical styles (always acoustic of course, with drums and guitars and fiddles and mandolins being most common) draw upon the style and legacy of the hippies. The clothing styles are also reminiscent of Grateful Dead concerts and the Haight-Ashbury culture: tie-dyes and flowing fabrics abound. These are not the values and choices of only those who actually lived through the 1960s counterculture; many younger folks adopt the values and practices of this culture of the so-called past as well.[17] But certainly not everyone at a Gathering fits this bill.

The "Dirty Kids"

I did not live through the counterculture of the 1960s, so I cannot say for certain how new the presence of "dirty kids" is in the counterculture or its representation at Rainbow Gatherings. Both young and old, there are many people at Rainbow Gatherings who do not identify with the colorful clothing and peaceful values of the hippies. They wear black and leather; they have multiple tattoos, sometimes covering their face; they hop trains and have big, aggressive-looking dogs. As Butterfly Bill writes,

> The popular image of a Rainbow gatherer had long been of a long-haired hippie dressed in colorful tie-dyes, with lots of Grateful Dead and Bob Marley logos. If a woman, she had on a granny dress and shawl with fringes and lots of jewelry. But for many years the gatherings had also been attended by an increasing number of people dressed in goth and punk rock outfits of black, brown, gray, and olive drab. They preferred heavy metal to psychedelic rock, and their concert tee shirts were almost always black. Lots of them were fond of body piercings and tattoos, and Mohawk hairdos were popular. Both the men and women liked military pants with lots of cargo pockets, with the legs either full length or cut off.[18]

The so-called dirty kids (who self-identify this way at Gatherings) are not necessarily kids at all, but they are an important group within the Rainbow Family. They are louder, gruffer, and more violent in speech and action than those who might be called hippies (whatever their age). After a call of "We love you!" through the dark woods, I've heard groups of dirty kids respond with yells of "We huff glue!" and then snicker uncontrollably. They look, act, and may even smell differently (scoffing at the scent of patchouli oil, popular among the hippies). But they come to gather for many of the same abstract reasons shared by other gatherers—to experience freedom, collective self-sufficiency, and noncommercialism—and they undoubtedly do much to contribute to the organization and culture of a Gathering.

The dirty kids often do not have jobs, homes, or traditional responsibilities in Babylon. Their lives are on the road, hitchhiking or train hopping or sharing old school buses. They are often the first to show up and the last to leave a Rainbow Gathering site, and they do a lot of the work necessary to create and dismantle this temporary world. Some of the kitchens are run exclusively by dirty kids;

at the 2012 National Gathering, Fat Kids kitchen was one of the first to have clean water and food to serve because they showed up as a whole crew of young people in three school buses ready to go just days after the site was announced. These folks often do a lot of the clean up at the end of the Gathering too. They haul bags of trash full of cigarette butts and other remains from campers long gone. They fill and bury shitters, dismantle kitchens, and make sure that the principles of leave-no-trace camping are put into practice for all those gatherers who didn't do it themselves.[19]

Many (but certainly not all) of the dirty kids are younger. Some of them present a real challenge to the vibe and culture of Rainbow. Some like to drink alcohol and sometimes violate the norm of keeping alcohol out of Rainbow land. For some, the values of peacefulness, environmental care, and spiritual connectivity simply do not resonate. Some do not honor the values of "peaceful respect,"[20] what others have called the only rule of Rainbow. Some do not want to join hands and Om before dinner, do yoga, or take nature walks. Some contradict the value of self-reliance held by many Rainbow Family participants[21] by "flying signs" (to ask for money) or "jugging" (to ask for gas), both in the parking lot and in nearby towns. In many ways, these young full-time travelers present a challenge, because they come in large numbers but do not always behave in the "Rainbow way." In a lot of other ways, the dirty kids are very important participants in the Family: they show up early and stay late, they organize kitchens, and they staff the parking lot security. They do a lot to contribute to a Gathering. They also challenge the Family to really put into practice the values of acceptance and freedom that are central to this ritual experience.

The Doers of Things

While walking down the trail chatting with a man named Fisher, who had just finished helping to install the water lines that run deep into the woods through the mountainous terrain to a source spring high above the Gathering and was now on his way to help clean a water filter at a kitchen, we passed a group of three men pulling and pushing a cart fully loaded with supplies up the trail. As we passed them, Fisher said, "Man, that guy is a mule! You see that guy with the big earrings? I've passed him carrying supplies four times today. I used to be like that. I've got back problems now, so I try to find ways to help that don't involve heavy loads." I recognized the man—shirtless and strong, with buzzed short black hair, multiple tattoos, and large holes in his ears filled with big metal plug earrings; I'd seen him three times that day myself, helping to haul in food, water, and other supplies. There are many like him at any Gathering—the doers of things. They spend their days working really hard, hauling heavy loads of anything for anyone who needs the assistance.

"Why do you think he does it?" I ask. "Or, why do you?" Fisher replied,

> It's a rush, you know, working your body like that. It's amazing to do things you didn't know you could. It's hard physical work; you feel strong. It's a total endorphin rush. That man's getting high off it. And to be able to see so directly how you're helping, most people never get that. Maybe that man spends most his time sitting on his couch selling bags of weed; instead he's out here helping people, working hard, and he gets that rush. I know I did.

Some people work incredibly hard at Rainbow Gatherings, seemingly busy all day long with physically demanding tasks. The people who do so, as Fisher suggests, may not be active participants in mainstream society. Yet at a Rainbow Gathering, they are often immediately rewarded with appreciation for their efforts with vocalized thanks and shouts of "Lovin' you!" At a Gathering, the reward for hard work does not come in the form of a paycheck or a promotion. Instead, it comes as acknowledgment and appreciation. For many gatherers, these rewards are worth more than any material reward offered by the systems of Babylon.

Gatherings literally could not happen without these active doers of things, who also contribute energetically to the Gathering experience of collectivity. Active participation in the systems required to meet the needs and comforts of all gatherers provides an emotional experience for those who participate, because they receive the vocally and energetically expressed thanks of the strangers who rely on their hard work. The doers of things also contribute to the emotional sense of connectivity experienced by the gatherers who are sitting around the campfire or wandering aimlessly down the trail who thank them aloud for their efforts. They are a reminder to all that everyone at a Gathering is connected, that everyone relies on the efforts of everyone else to create the unique social world they inhabit together. Because of the doers of things, ritualized interactions of love and appreciation—where people say "thank you" and "lovin' you, brother" or "lovin' you, sister" to the strangers working hard to make their world possible—a routine aspect of the Rainbow Gathering experience, contribute to the emotional high experienced by many of those who gather.

Bliss Ninnies, Freeloaders, and Drainbows

During a visit to Twin Oaks, an egalitarian income-sharing community (a commune) in Virginia, one of the longtime residents there told me,

> You know, Rainbow is the only place that does it better than we do. And by that I mean, we are able to meet everybody's needs here, but we can't afford any freeloaders. Everybody has to put into the system in order for us to keep the system going. But at Rainbow, a few are able to meet the needs of the many. Some people work really hard, other people don't do a damn thing, but everyone still gets fed.

There are a lot of people at Rainbow Gatherings who don't do anything "productive" during their time in the woods. Some are what a friend of mine calls "the fucking freeloaders"—people who will ask you for anything and everything ("Can I have a cigarette? Do you have any water? How about an extra pair of shoes?") without ever considering how they could help contribute to the functioning of a Gathering. There is even a specific term for these folks at a Rainbow Gathering: "drainbows." They are the folks who come with nothing and rely entirely on community resources without giving anything back.

Sometimes it's amazing to see how people react to being in a space where their needs will be met (if they're hungry, they will be freely fed; if they're thirsty, they will find free clean water; and if they smoke, they will be given cigarettes)—some people will just ask for anything! This isn't true only of those who might be judged as freeloaders in mainstream society. I've seen young men who appear to be local college students, in clean, brand-name clothing, clean-cut hairstyles, and backwards baseball caps, get so into it that they too are asking for everything, even though they'll return home in the evening. There are also those that just seem so "blissed out"—so high, either literally or just metaphorically, relishing in the energy of the Gathering—that they don't ever get up to dig a shitter, build a campfire, fetch firewood, or carry water.

These so-called "bliss ninnies" arguably contribute to the Gathering in other ways, however. Some wander the trails giving free hugs to anyone who accepts the offer; some start group hugs whenever they wander by a willing group; some find each other and sit holding hands and smiling. I once saw a man and woman so blissed out that they sat cross-legged facing each other, holding hands and smiling silently, uninterrupted for a whole day. While they didn't feed people or help keep them hydrated, they provided a reason to smile, a reason to recognize the bliss that others were feeling, and perhaps a reason for others to feel a little bit of it in themselves.

The First-Timers

At the 2012 National Gathering, I met a young man in his late teens or early twenties who called himself Mickey. He and three other young men had stopped to take a break from pushing a cart loaded heavy with boxes of food up a steep trail. I stopped to say thank you to them as I passed, and Mickey immediately started chatting.

"Hey, thank you, we're doing this for all of us, you know, working hard and laboring for love. What's your name?" I told him.

"I'm Mickey. This is my first Rainbow Gathering. Got here two days ago, and man, I mean, sorry, I'm having a blast!" (Some folks at Rainbow Gatherings discourage gendered language, although there are certainly no formalized rules of speech. Mickey was just learning this, of course.)

"It's nice to meet you, Mickey," I say, our eyes still connected. "How did you learn about this Gathering?"

"Well, I heard about them a few months ago, and I just couldn't wait to get here. As soon as I knew where it was going to be, I caught a ride out of Florida. Don't know if I'll ever go back."

"Well, welcome home," I said. "And again, thank you all!"

I got a round of "Lovin' you, sister" from the four men before wandering off. A short time later, they made it to their destination, a kitchen where I was already sitting and chatting with other gatherers. Mickey, seeing a familiar face, came up to join us right away.

"Hi, I'm Mickey," he said to the three other folks I was sitting with. "Can I join you?"

"Of course," we all said.

"Wow, thanks. This is my first time, and I sure love this Rainbow Gathering."

One of the folks sitting with us, a woman who had noticed him helping with the food delivery, responded, "And this Rainbow Gathering loves you!"

That afternoon, I saw Mickey all over the place—helping to bring supplies up the trail, chatting it up with folks at four different kitchens, sitting among the traders at trade circle. He is, in my experience, a typical first-timer. For most people, the first time they experience a Rainbow Gathering is like no other.

It really is like entering a whole new world. For those who have been looking for a kinder, more welcoming, and less consumer-driven existence, it can feel like coming home for the first time. Thrilled to be in a space where everyone is open to conversation, they talk to absolutely everyone. Seeing tangibly and immediately how appreciated their efforts are, they work hard, jumping at every chance to volunteer. They stay up all night, sometimes for multiple nights in a row, enthralled by the campfires and the music and the magic. They are excited; their energy seems endless. They radiate.

It would be impossible to say how many first-timers come back to a second or third or tenth or twentieth Gathering. I would guess that there are a lot of first-timers at every Gathering who never make it back "home," as the Gathering moves to new locations every year and thus geography, opportunity, and people's lives change. A lot of first-timers are young, of course, especially given the population of runaways and other young kids who end up on the streets and then in the woods at a Rainbow Gathering. A lot of first-timers, however, are not young. Many have jobs and homes and lives outside of Rainbow, although some do not. No matter their age or circumstance outside of Rainbow, these first-timers are important contributors to any Rainbow Gathering. First of all, their physical energy and excitement mean that they get a lot done. Second, and perhaps more important, they contribute to the emotional energy of the Gathering. My friend really meant it when she told Mickey, "This Rainbow Gathering loves you!" Her energy was heightened by his excitement; this energy was then passed along through other interactions. Excitement is contagious, after all, and the excited first-timers who really get into the vibe help to perpetuate the positivity. Their contribution to the collective is felt and further contributes in a way that helps maintain the energy of the Gathering itself.

Locals

Many first-timers are locals, people who live in nearby towns who come to the Gathering. Because the Gathering moves to a new location each year and always gets a little notice in the local press, there are different local residents who come every year, either to party in the woods[22] or to gawk at the crazy-looking hippies and freaks who are.[23] I met a few first-timers at the Tennessee Gathering who had heard about it through an article in the local paper.[24] Some locals simply drive down the parking lot road, never actually walking into the Gathering. At the 2012 National Gathering in Tennessee, I saw seemingly hundreds of cars with Sullivan County plates driving by, some with wide-eyed drivers waving enthusiastically. When I wanted to reach the main entrance more quickly, I caught a ride with one of the many locals who cruised the parking lot road giving rides and saying hello to all the unusual folks who had come to inhabit the National Forest. During a slow two-and-a-half-mile drive down a dusty gravel road crowded with lingering people, barking dogs, and cars attempting to come or go, we talked about the Gathering. This man seemed to be deeply touched by the Rainbow experience, even though he had only seen the parking lot.

Locals may come in and walk around for a day; others camp overnight, and some stay longer. Locals are almost always identifiable, sometimes by accents (depending on the location) but more typically by their mainstream style and clean clothing, hair, and selves. Although they may not get as actively involved as the typical first-timer, their rapture with the experience is usually pretty similar. Many unmistakably get into the energetic experience of the Gathering, even if they come for only a short time. Walking down a trail at the National Gathering in Tennessee, I saw a local man and woman—both heavy-set and middle-aged, wearing clean jean shorts and tennis shoes, wide-eyed and holding hands—wandering toward me.

"Good morning! Welcome home!" I said with a smile.

"Hello," she tentatively replied. It seems I was not the first person to make eye contact and share a vocal greeting, but she didn't yet seem sure of an appropriate response. "How are you?"

"Fabulous," I said. "And how are you?"

"Good, and how are you?" she blurted out before realizing she was repeating herself and gave me a sheepish grin. I gave her a wide smile, and we passed. In mainstream society, these sorts of exchanges are rare and perfunctory. When was the last time a complete stranger looked you in the eye, asked how you were, and genuinely hoped for a response? It's no wonder she seemed a little shaken by it, I thought to myself as I continued wandering, saying hello to the other smiling faces more accustomed to Rainbow ways.

Later that afternoon, I walked back to the parking lot to retrieve a flashlight. As I reached my car, a man stopped me and shook my hand.

"Hello, how are you?" he said with a friendly smile.

"I'm great," I told him. "How are you?"

"Doing real good," he said, and he continued on, shaking hands with each person he passed. As I headed back up the road toward the main trail, I saw him stop and chat with a group of men with dreadlocks next to a painted bus.

They were explaining to him what "Six up" and "Seven up" mean; "Six up" had just driven by.

"Six up is the police, man," one of the guys told him, with an emphasis on the "po" rather than the "lice." "That's how we communicate with our Family that the cops is rolling through and it's time to be careful. Seven up is a newer thing, I think, and that's the Forest Service. 'Cause you know, they aren't gonna arrest you."

"Oh, I see, fascinating," the man replied. "What else?"

Then I realized why that man had shaken my hand rather than given me a hug or simply a smile. I can hear it in his accent. He's a local. Excited by all the communication and contact, he started doing the only type of touching he was used to doing with strangers—shaking hands. As I continue my walk up the trail, I hope that he'll make it through the parking lot and into the Gathering, imagining how excited he might be then.

The Forest Service rangers and local law enforcement are another category of locals (although some Forest Service rangers travel from across the country to work at the Gathering year after year) who experience the Rainbow Gathering, albeit in a different way. The Rainbow Family attempts to avoid interactions with law enforcement, preferring to handle Family issues internally through "Shanti Sena"—the voluntary peacekeepers of the Gathering who are called to intervene when issues arise.[25] Nonetheless, "Six up" (law enforcement) and "Seven up" (Forest Service resource managers; I'm told the language differentiates between officers who are carrying guns and those who are not) are a daily, almost constant presence at a Gathering. It seems like these identifying calls echo through the woods more than a dozen times each day. Local law enforcement officers make occasional arrests, but since the National Forest is under their jurisdiction, the Forest Service is the more powerful and responsible entity of the state at a Gathering. They walk through the Gathering often; they interact with kitchens and other camps, enforcing rules (like those restricting camping near a water source) and making suggestions.

In their own ways, Forest Service rangers and law enforcement officials are participants in the social world of a Rainbow Gathering, shaping as well as being shaped by the experience. When rangers want to communicate with the entire Family, they are asked to attend the daily council, where they sit in a circle and listen to others as they wait for their turn to hold the feather that's passed around to indicate a speaker's turn. They even participate by hanging signs throughout the woods to inform and communicate with gatherers (theirs are identifiable because they are printed and hanging in protective plastic sleeves rather than painted by hand on cardboard).[26]

Focalizers and Facilitators: The "Hi Holies"

While there is no formal organization of the Rainbow Family of the Living Light or any official hierarchy at a Rainbow Gathering, there are certainly people who take an organizational role in making Gatherings happen. These facilitators avoid words like leader and leadership (though some refer to them, somewhat derogatorily, as the "Hi Holies"), but they essentially provide leadership-type direction and planning. Many of the elders are heavily involved in councils (the consensus-based decision-making bodies of Rainbow) and site selection (the scouting of National Forests for future sites). Other facilitating/leadership roles include coordination and purchasing of supplies and managing relations with the Forest Service, local law enforcement, and the press. As Butterfly Bill argues, the ways that facilitators, focalizers, and "not-supposed-to-call-them-leaders" help get things done serve as an "example of how leadership could be embraced as benevolent rather than feared as punishing. The anarchy of the gathering revealed basic traits of character in people that others learned to recognize and appreciate."[27]

It is important to the spirit of the Rainbow Family that no one speaks for anyone else, so those that play focalizing and facilitating roles should not be considered spokespersons for the Family. However, a lot needs to get done to make a Gathering happen. Each year, a "Vision Council" is held at the end of the National Gathering, where attendees agree by consensus to organize a Gathering for the next year and choose potential locations. Elders and other people heavily involved in their regional Rainbow Family networks attend, as well as many others. Sometimes these meetings go on for days.

Then, the following spring, a specific site must be chosen. Scouts go out and look at all potential sites (in the area agreed to at the Vision Council), and a spring council convenes in early June to decide on the exact location. Once a site is chosen, kitchens arrive to set up, and all sorts of logistics—from relations with Forest Service resource rangers and local police to the location of shitters and water lines to the source of food for Main Supply to the distribution of funds from the Magic Hat—must be dealt with quickly, because the crowds start coming shortly after the site is announced.

During main circle, the Magic Hat is passed around to collect cash donations for Main Supply—you can also donate to the Magic Hat by stopping at Information. This is the only way money is intended to enter the world of Rainbow. A banking council handles the money, dispensing it to the Main Supply drivers who go into town to buy supplies, which are brought back to Main Supply and then distributed to the kitchens.

Focalizers and facilitators are extremely important to the continuation and success of these annual events. These rituals could not take place without those who participate in selecting the site; running kitchens; obtaining and organizing supplies; serving as mediators between the local community (including law enforcement) and the Family; facilitating communication within the Family through councils, committees, and Shanti Sena (the peacekeepers); and helping with the many other organizational tasks involved in creating and maintaining this incredibly unique, temporary social world.

It is also true that in a world where no one is officially appointed or assigned any position and no codified leadership structure exists and in which people are able—in fact encouraged—to participate and communicate openly, there is sometimes friction between those who act as or are identified by others as facilitators and those who only self-identify as such. Sometimes people get high on their newly perceived importance and consider themselves in charge of a certain task or start telling others what to do. These people often quickly find themselves without volunteers to carry out their orders. The focalizer or facilitator role is often fluid and shifting, and sometimes mistaken and contested.

Furthermore, although many who act in a facilitating or focalizing role often seem very busy, there is a division between those who do and those who organize. My friend Jackson told me that he prefers to do whatever needs to be done and often prefers to be told how he can help, although his favorite kitchen task to take on is cooking (one that often needs very little organizational direction at a Gathering) because he likes to cook outside. In contrast, he says that his friend Lazy is a great focalizer and organizer, but "he's definitely not the one to jump on actually doing something."

Similarly, when I asked an elder facilitator at another kitchen about their water source, he said, "I know it's up the hill somewhere, but I haven't actually gone to get water. I trust that it's working and working well; the crew seems to leave to get water and come back with water, so it must be there." This man had been involved with this kitchen for decades; he was very involved in choosing the site for the kitchen at the Gathering and was always around to encourage volunteers or organize tasks, but he was not actively involved in the daily operating procedures that require physical work.

Many of the focalizers and facilitators at Rainbow are elders, but this seems to be shifting slowly. At the 2012 National Gathering, I heard one older focalizer talking to another about how happy he was to see younger people involved in all of the organizational roles at this Gathering, from the Magic Hat collection to the establishment of the water supply to the information booth. At this most recent Gathering, there were also several kitchens with younger men and women serving in facilitating roles.[28] Teddy, who is younger than many of the other facilitators, has been an active participant at Rainbow Gatherings since his first one five years ago. He told me that five Family elders who were actively involved facilitators had died in the past year (2011–2012) and that some of the elders have started actively looking for participatory younger gatherers to take under their wings and help them get more involved. He said he could clearly see younger people getting more involved in the organizational tasks at the past few Gatherings. A slow generational shift, necessary for the sustainability of the Family and its Gatherings, is occurring among those who take on focalizing and facilitating roles within the Rainbow Family.[29]

Angry Drunks

Many Rainbow Family participants would likely agree that while marijuana and hallucinogenic drugs are medicinal, spiritual, or in some other way beneficial, alcohol is nothing but poison. Most are against alcohol usage in general and are vehemently against it at a Gathering, believing that the use of alcohol often provokes behavior that is in contradiction with the peaceful intentions of the Gathering. Natural substances that do not create a lot of trash—such as roll-your-own tobacco, marijuana, and hallucinogenic mushrooms—are much more accepted. Rainbow Gatherings have been alcohol-free since the very beginning, and an old man with a long beard wearing nothing but a colorful robe who calls himself Woodstock told me that alcohol "wasn't at the first Gathering and it shouldn't be at any of them." I once heard an elder Family member say, "Keep your alcohol in the parking lot; this is our church!" But in reality, a lot of alcohol is consumed at Rainbow Gatherings.

Alcohol consumption is often associated with violence at a Gathering. One night early on in the 2012 Gathering, the police breaking up a domestic dispute woke me up from my sleep in the RV in the parking lot; a drunken couple had been fighting violently. The next day, however, the local paper still reported that "no incidences" had occurred at the Gathering. I wondered if the Family was able to keep the police from getting involved formally; gatherers prefer to keep the police out as much as possible, handling things as a Family rather than bringing in Babylonian law enforcement. I have heard many other Gathering stories of police altercations and violent incidences, some resulting in hospital-ization, where alcohol was involved.

Yet nondrinking gatherers treat most of the drinkers and the violence that often results from alcohol abuse with calm consideration. The cultural value of peacefulness becomes less important than the value of freedom when it comes to dealing with real human beings, albeit drunk, angry, violent ones—a minority at most Gatherings most of the time, to be sure—who make their own choices. Many gatherers believe that a greater peace is served by responding to alcohol consumption and its consequences with love and compassion rather than anger and rejection. Most drinkers respect the spatial division between "A-camp," the very first camping area adjacent to the parking lot and front gate, where alcohol consumption is accepted, and Rainbow land. And most drinkers are not violent toward others, particularly outside A-camp. As one young dirty kid who had recently gotten yelled at for drinking inside the Gathering told me, "Rainbow is about accommodating all kinds of people and habits. If I can respect their space and not be belligerent, then they should respect mine. But I guess I'm on my way back down to the parking lot." Talking about the alcoholics who come to Gatherings and spend all their time in A-camp, a longtime Rainbow Family participant and Vietnam veteran named Chip told me, "They're Family too, and they're good people. We all have a place here."

One of the most foundational values for the Rainbow Family is freedom, and with that freedom comes acceptance. There are at least a few possible ex-planations for the relatively peaceful acceptance of alcohol and violence, both of which violate the spirit and intentions of the Rainbow Family. One is that the angriest and most violent of these drinkers usually do keep it in the parking lot, arguably preferring to hang out with like-minded gatherers. Another is that they really do help the Family by managing traffic in the parking lot and operating as a security force, albeit with their own sort of flavor. A third is that many of these Family members have known each other and interacted for years, and they have a relationship despite their differences. As Jackson told me of his A-camp friend Doc, "He's a great guy and I really love him. He is violent for sure and I prefer not to hang out too much, but I love him." On a more abstract level, the spirituality (one that claims to recognize connectivity and oneness) and openness of Rainbow culture encourage this sort of tolerance, encourage the active pursuit of both peacefulness and freedom. One young man explained his feelings toward the presence of angry drunks at the Gathering in this way: "There's a duality, you know. Good and bad, light and darkness. We need both the darkness and the light."

Sisters and Mamas: Women at Rainbow

Women, of course, fall into all of the categories above: They pray, participate, fight, and focalize. But they share a unique experience at the Gathering. While men are called "brother," women are called "sister" or "mama"—and all sisters and mamas experience particular aspects of Rainbow culture in ways that are different from their brothers. The Rainbow Family has, according to some, long struggled with gender dynamics and gender equality.[30] Although Rainbow Gatherings have always espoused peaceful, nonviolent, and respectful forms of communication and action, some of the male-dominated behavior that occurs at a Gathering is nothing short of predatory.

The open and expressive culture of a Gathering is sometimes applied to intimate or sexual relationships, as the "test" I saw at Information (see Figure 1.1) suggested. This is sometimes made perverse by the ways men very actively and eagerly attempt to meet women, sometimes half their age or even younger. I met one woman at the 2012 Gathering who had let her fifteen-year-old daughter bring her boyfriend along to the Gathering. When someone else questioned her decision, she said, "At least this way I know she won't have to deal with some of the dirty old men around here who would be hitting on her." I also met a man wandering the trail looking for his girlfriend who said he was concerned about finding her "because of all the creeps around here." He said that, knowing how men looked at and talked to her with him around, he couldn't imagine what it was like without his presence.

This, of course, opens many moral boxes. I do not mean to imply that there are rapists running loose in the woods, and I do not mean to downplay a woman's own agency to choose whose flirtations and company she enjoys (an issue further complicated by the fact that some of these women are actually underage girls). The important thing is to note that some parts of Rainbow culture that contribute to the positive energy of the event—open communication, freedom of expression, anonymity, and connectivity—actually also contribute to a shared experience among the women at Gatherings that is often sexist, degrading, and somewhat predatory.

Not-Wellness

There are folks that come to Rainbow Gatherings—a minority for sure, but arguably a significant one—that are simply not well, for one reason or another.

Some seem to suffer from mental and emotional trauma; for many of the veterans, this is explainable by their profession. Some of the angry drunks and other types of substance abusers are likely not well psychologically or emotionally. Some of the people you meet may seem out of touch with reality, as you know it. Listen to enough stories, and you're also likely to meet an outlaw or criminal or two. These folks certainly color some of the conversations or experiences you might have at a Gathering.

Yet the difference between Babylon and a Rainbow Gathering is arguably not the extent to which physical dependencies, emotional instabilities, psychological abnormalities, or criminal tendencies exist but the openness with which they are expressed, conveyed, or shared—and accepted—as a part of the freedom to be (and to be loved). As Michael Niman writes of the Rainbow Family, it

> has its share . . . of child predators, rapists, muggers, and thieves. Members acknowledge that whatever's "out there" in Babylon is also "in here" at Gatherings. The Family is, after all, a microcosm of the greater society. What sets the Family apart from American municipal authorities is that while both face violent and disruptive individuals, they respond differently. Rainbows confront violence and hate with peace and love.[31]

Types without Stereotypes: A Family of Individuals

There are so many people from so many different walks of life at a Gathering. Some are young, others old. Some are highly educated, while others are not. Some travel for thousands of miles to attend; others come just because it's close to wherever they call home. Some people come for a day; some for a week; still others are at the National Gathering site for six weeks or more, from the very beginning to the very end. Some spend the rest of their years living a sedentary, homebound life working full-time, while others travel year round.[32]

Although the Rainbow Gathering is idealistically about a prayer for peace, not all those who attend are praying. One of the unique things about Rainbow is that they don't have to be in order to be welcome. The freedom to be—to be kind or cranky, to be compassionate or belligerent—trumps the importance of being peaceful. This freedom bordering on anarchy is "an expression. Acting together without leaders [is] itself a statement about how we think people could and should live."[33]

This is one of the hardest things to understand about the Rainbow Family—how a group of people who are seeking peaceful communion by gathering together can also be accepting of those who do not choose peace. At a Gathering, being tolerant becomes more important than being peaceful, because it is the only way to truly demonstrate a peaceful acceptance and a welcoming freedom. It takes all types of folks to bring this temporary village together and make it come alive with the emotional energy of collective effervescence.

At the 2012 National Gathering, I saw a sign along the trail that read: "Let us learn to respect until we can learn to love." The communal vibe that you feel at a Gathering is not that of perfection but pursuit of absolute acceptance. An elder who calls himself Grandpa put it this way: "The drainest of the drainbows and the highest of the holies, we all need each other and are all a part of this Family."

CHAPTER 3
RAINBOW LAND

UNDERSTANDING RAINBOW SPACE

The 2012 National Rainbow Gathering was held in the very northeastern corner of Tennessee, and I arrived just a few days after the site had been announced on the unofficial Rainbow Family website[1] and more than two weeks before the Gathering officially began. I'd come to the Gathering with my partner, Dave, and following the directions we'd found online, we drove down a Forest Service road until we wondered whether we'd gone too far. After continuing on in hesitation for a few more minutes we rounded a corner and saw a colorfully painted school bus parked off the road, an indication that we had found our way home.

We drove slowly past the small line of parked cars until we reached a man with dark hair and a big dark beard, likely in his early twenties, wearing a black t-shirt and a neon orange crossing guard–style vest that said "Sanitation" on the back. Who knows where the vest had come from, but it was a good indication that this man was "working the front gate" and was there to welcome us home. When we stopped to talk to him, he said, "Welcome home," and told us in a gruff voice that our best bet was to turn around and park in the line of cars. He said, "No parking on that side of the street." Bright orange "No Parking" signs were attached to the trees on that side and it was clear from the other cars that parking was only allowed on one side of the road (a rule put in place and enforced by the Forest Service specifically for the Gathering); but he made sure to tell us anyway. He also said, "Make sure all four tires are off the road. So be careful where you park, because there's not enough space for that in some places." With this welcoming and instruction, we turned around to find a spot.

There were already eighty-two cars and eight school buses parked in the "parking lot"—a Rainbow term for wherever cars are parked, whether it be an actual lot or simply a long row of cars on the side of a road. There was one small open area where large buses pulled completely off the road into their own little lot. This early, only a few kitchens were fully established and operable. Nevertheless, even early in the Gathering, the physical space was already organized in a way familiar to me. Although they've been in very different places (the Upper Peninsula of Michigan, northern California, West Virginia, Colorado, Wyoming, and Tennessee) with very different landscapes, every National Gathering I've attended has had a relatively similar organization of space.

In describing the Chicago school of sociology, Andrew Abbott remarks, "Throughout the Chicago writings, we find time and place."[2] This chapter brings the ecological focus of the Chicago school to the study of Rainbow Gatherings, focusing on spatial organization, the interactional processes through which spatial organization emerges, and the patterns of social-spatial relationships.[3] Rainbow Gatherings are a social world unfamiliar to many Americans, composed of what seem like atypical individuals and unusual forms of (dis)organization; such "deviant scenes . . . often appear disorganized to the uninitiated outsider."[4] However, "inherent in every social world is a system of social organization."[5] The spatial patterns that emerge at each Rainbow Gathering are both conditions and symbols of the human relationships that emerge in this social world,[6] as the processes of organizing and using space are themselves part of the ritual.

Negotiated Order and Patterned Anarchy in the Organization of Rainbow Space

The spatial organization of a Rainbow Gathering is spontaneous, ever-evolving, and quite anarchistic. It "is not . . . an absolute space but a complexly contoured, somewhat permeable but none the less bounded landscape which . . . must possess a specific configuration of minimal requirements."[7] Other than some simple restrictions based on carefully using and interacting with the land (e.g., keeping camps, kitchens, and shitters away from water sources) and a handful of physical requirements (a place for cars to park; a water source that can be captured, transported through water lines, and filtered for drinking; a meadow large enough to hold the evening meals and main circle on July 4), any space can be used by anyone for any purpose at any time. In this anarchistic social world where no one is "in charge" of organizing or mediating the use of space, spatial order is negotiated[8] as real people with real interests[9] interact to establish their campsites, kitchens, and spaces for activities. Through interpersonal interaction, a negotiated order shapes the pattern of spatial organization at a Gathering, where there is order "within the apparent disorganization."[10]

The patterned organization of physical space at a Rainbow Gathering emerges, evolves, and disappears quickly to accommodate all those who gather in this temporary social world. At the 2012 National Gathering, the local press reported 600 people in attendance by June 19, 700 attendees on June 22, and a population height of an estimated 6,500–7,500 by July 4 (and this was a very small National Gathering). By July 6 there were an estimated 4,700 people left at the Gathering, and only 300–400 by July 15.[11] In just a few short weeks, a remote section of National Forest land is transformed into a temporary metropolis with hundreds of cars parked on miles of road, thousands of feet traveling miles of trails, miles of water line running through the woods, dozens of kitchens and fire pits and latrines and earthen ovens, more daily events than one individual could possibly attend, a medical facility, an information booth, hundreds of campsites, and a multitude of signs pointing the way to various places, services, and happenings.

Every site chosen for a Rainbow Gathering, and thus the specific spatial organization of every event, is different. Yet there is a pattern that reemerges year after year, a pattern that evolves spontaneously in direct relationship with the physical landscape of the site. There is, of course, contestation over spatial organization. At the 2002 National Gathering in the Upper Peninsula of Michigan, the Forest Service deemed one half of the site a sensitive archeological site (old mining remains were found by the gatherers who showed up early) and restricted camps to one side of a river that ran through the middle of the site. A handful of gatherers were arrested in a standoff over the use of the space, but in the end the Gathering took place on half of the expected site. At the 2012 Gathering, parking was restricted to one side of a wide gravel Forest Service road (understandably to ensure that cars could still pass one another) and there was no centrally located parking; some people had to park miles from either of the two main entries (here dubbed "front gate" and "not front gate"), just to walk another mile or two into the Gathering. In response, some gatherers created an impromptu shuttle service during the busiest days of the Gathering. The organization emerges spontaneously, but only through the interaction of real people and real landscapes as they negotiate[12] and actively participate in acts of space-shaping.

Yet every year the physical space of the National Rainbow Gathering becomes a patterned city in the woods as people spontaneously participate in processes of spatial organization. No official organizing body or leadership team makes these organizational choices; individual people interact to negotiate, collaborate, communicate, and cooperate in the organization of this temporary space. Here I'd like you to take a walk with me through the 2012 National Gathering as we talk about the spatial arrangement of the Gathering.

The Parking Lot, Front Gate, and A-Camp

We arrived at the Gathering in Tennessee on June 15, and Dave and I didn't leave the parking lot on the day we arrived. We watched and listened as the folks at "front gate" greeted newly arriving gatherers before instructing them to find a parking spot along the road before they unloaded their camping supplies and set off down the trail. Front gate serves an interestingly functional purpose at the Gathering. First of all, there's always someone there to welcome new arrivals and help give them directions for parking and hiking in. Perhaps more interesting: alcohol is discouraged in Rainbow land, yet drinking is tolerated in the parking lot, around the front gate, and in the camping space immediately next to the front gate called A-camp. Although it may seem slightly dysfunctional, the alcohol drinkers help to patrol others coming into the Gathering; I've heard many stories of people having beer confiscated on the way up the trail by A-campers who tell them that they're not allowed to drink in Rainbow land.[13] The often drunk and sometimes violent people at front gate and A-camp serve the Gathering by welcoming people, giving them parking instructions, and running security by seeing everyone who arrives; these spaces provide a place where people who like to get drunk can (and do) without imposing on those who prefer the no-alcohol norm of Rainbow land.

That first night in Tennessee, Dave and I hung out with a man who had spent the past five years working the front gate at National Gatherings. He told us, "I'm excited to be working a kitchen this year, so I won't be drinking. I spent five years getting drunk so that the hippies in the woods could play their drums and have a good time in peace and safety. I dealt with all the dirty street kids coming through who wouldn't respect that, who were causing all sorts of trouble, so that they didn't have to."

The people who voluntarily work the front gate (who call themselves "front gaters"—I once even saw a man working front gate wearing a "Gator" hat, a plush alligator sitting atop his head, as a sort of mascot) are often drunk, loud, gruff, and harsh, just the type you want working security. It means that alcohol drinkers also have a place that they are welcome, and it means that they get there before they wander up into the Gathering where most people are uncomfortable with drinking. As Mama Renee told me, "They have their job to do, and they do it well." In other words, "many 'A' Campers often work hard at Gatherings when they're not drunk and are on the front lines when abusive locals or authorities try to harass the Gathering. Hence they deserve respect and understanding."[14]

Rainbow Land

"Rainbow land" starts after you have left the parking lot, passed front gate, and walked past A-camp. Continuing down the "main trail" (the common term for whatever pathway, often a pre-existing hiking trail, is used to connect the front gate and parking lot to the main Gathering space at any given site), the entrance into Rainbow land is only noticeable by the sounds and sights around you. Still in the same woods, the vibe changes, and you are "home."

As Dave and I walked down the trail with our camping gear the next morning, other gatherers looked us in the eye and said, "Welcome home." Even then, over two weeks before the official beginning of the Gathering, tents spotted the landscape, some right next to the main trail, some hidden off in the woods. Kitchens—where food is made over campfires or in earthen ovens and where people are fed for free—were few and far between this early in the Gathering, but there would be dozens soon.

Water from a natural spring or clean stream is carried through long systems of PVC piping for miles and miles around the Gathering site to provide water as close to kitchens as possible. Kitchens provide drinking water to attendees, often in "water buffaloes" (large tanks of filtered water) located on a kitchen's "bliss rail" (makeshift countertop). Drinking water stations are often also situated throughout the Gathering. All water is filtered or boiled before use (unless an individual gatherer chooses to drink directly from the source, which is highly discouraged). How much water is available and how many resources there are for piping, filtering, and providing water vary from year to year, depending on the site and what supplies the people who attend provide. An occasional attendee will bring a large water cistern with them on a trailer or in the back of a pickup truck to share with other gatherers, especially if the chosen site doesn't have plentiful water available.

In addition to a natural spring or clean stream, sites chosen for Rainbow Gatherings sometimes have a "swimming hole"—a river, pond, or lake where people can bathe. People sometimes set up solar showers as well, heavy black plastic containers filled with water that you can stand under, or even just simple PVC piping hung high in the air with an opening at the end serving as a spout pouring water, especially if natural bathing options are scarce, dirty, or cold.

"Shitter digging" is usually organized and executed by the kitchens. You can always find a shitter by asking at a kitchen; they are usually located nearby (but not too near), tucked back in the woods down small trails, typically indicated with signs or bright things tied to tree branches. Although the right location for a shitter always has to be decided on site, the spatial organization of shitters and kitchens has been consistent across decades of Gatherings.

The same can be said of the locations for the kitchens themselves—although each kitchen chooses its own spot in a site that is different every year, there are certain general tendencies for spatial arrangement. The kitchens that bring food to serve at main circle are typically clustered pretty close to the main meadow so that they don't have to trek the food too far. Kitchens that make incredibly appealing food like pizza and doughnuts are often at the far reaches of Rainbow land; the long hike helps avert the high demand that might otherwise be overwhelming. Although there are children all over Rainbow land, integrated and participating in a way that is unique when compared with the age segregation in Babylon, there is always a child-friendly space called Kid Village where families can be surrounded by other children and parents for constant play and support, and Kid Village is typically fairly centrally located and is always a good distance from A-camp.

Some kitchens make only tea, others only coffee, and they are usually dispersed throughout the Gathering. Kitchens have campfires called "bliss pits," separate from cook fires, where people can hang out, converse, and play music in close range of their tents and anything that needs done in a kitchen. Personal campfires are highly discouraged. Because people hang out around kitchen campfires, kitchens can shout out for volunteers to help and always have several ears within shouting distance. One of the benefits of being connected to (volunteering with and working hard for) a kitchen—sometimes described as being on a kitchen's "crew"—is that many of the "kick-downs" of treats from chocolate and Gatorade to marijuana, mushrooms, and acid go to kitchens.

Our second day in Tennessee, Dave and I walked the entire Gathering. We wandered down a dirt trail through an incredible forest with magnolia trees blooming all around us until we reached a T intesection. Turning left, we quickly reached main meadow, very centrally located at this Gathering (it often is, although we humans—specifically these nomadic humans using public land—of course have no control over the location of a meadow). The information booth (which provides Rainbow Gathering literature such as the "mini-manual," printed copies of the "raps" and the Rainbow paper "All Ways Free," a bulletin board of notes from people looking for one another and ride shares offered and needed after the Gathering, a lost-and-found, and an ever-evolving map, among other things) is also usually somewhere near the middle of it all, although it wasn't set up yet on this early walk through Rainbow land. We continued further down and after a long walk, we reached the end of the trail at Montana Mud, a kitchen known for its coffee (referred to exclusively as mud). Making our way back and continuing past the T, we passed a few more kitchens, went another mile or so before we saw Kid Village setting up, and then hiked another few miles along a loop back to the parking lot. I knew that this space would become much more congested as more and more Family arrived over the next days and weeks. How different would the space look as it filled up?

By July 3, Rainbow land was crowded with kitchens and camps and folks of all sorts. People seemed to pour in constantly for two days; the space occupied by parked cars seemed to multiply exponentially. The woods became absolutely packed with tents, fire pits, hung tarps, water lines, dogs, cats, pet birds, one pet pig, and people. The trails were literally worn slick, exposing bare rock underneath or turning into mud soup after several days of afternoon rain and the trampling of thousands of boots, shoes, bare feet, and dog paws.

In the few weeks that I had been there, I had visited and seen an amazing assortment of camps. The dirty kids were located at one end of the Gathering and had several kitchens—Fat Kids, Montana Mud, Shut Up and Eat It—and several camps—Goat Camp, Nic at Night, and the Ludest Temple among them. I also visited Fairy Camp, a kitchen organized by and providing space for gay, lesbian, queer, transgendered, androgynous, polyamorous, and allied folks (at this kitchen, they yell, "Yoo-hoo!" in high-pitched voices when food is being served, instead of the typical "Free food in the woods!"). I had seen the Jewish camp Home Shalom, Jesus Kitchen, and the Hare Krishna Kitchen. There are many other kitchens, like Iris, Kick Down Café, Musical Veggie, Magic Bowl, and Magic Bean. There is Pop Corner (for popcorn), Lovin' Ovens (they make pizza), kitchens that only serve

Figures 3.1 and 3.2: Two pictures of the main meadow at the 2012 Gathering, one side undisturbed and the other totally trampled after over a week of main circle meals and activities. Taken on July 8. *Source:* Chelsea Schelly.

coffee (like Crazy Cowboy's Coffee Corner), others that serve only tea (Tea Time), and the elaborate stage of the Granola Funk Theater. I had seen a primitive skills camp, a "quiet camp," a hammock camp called Safe Swinging, and a camp—clearly a reference to one particular section on the website craigslist.org—called Casual Encounterz. I have seen a Shaman's Corner, a medicine wheel (a circular space set aside for prayer and meditation), a yoga camp, and a sweat lodge.

Miles of trail had been developed through these woods; some were here before and are now much more worn, but many are new, made by gatherers themselves. This year, the trade "circle" was set up right along main trail, right at the busiest intersection, so that it wasn't a circle at all but instead just a long line of blankets covered with tradeable goods on either side of the trail. Main meadow, which began full of blackberry bushes, was completely trampled (see Figures 3.1 and 3.2).

Participatory Space-Making

The spatial organization of a Rainbow Gathering happens through the active participation, interaction, and negotiation of gatherers themselves. The size and success of each kitchen can fluctuate from year to year, often based on the assets, resources, and challenges provided in the specific context of physical space and spatial organization of the Gathering. The landscape and spatial organization of the Gathering, which change every year, influence the size and style of each kitchen in any given year. The 2011 National Gathering in Washington was incredibly wet and the site incredibly swampy, but Montana Mud set up at a high and dry point, so it became a popular place to hang out and there were people there all the time. They were hoping for a similar scene in 2012, a populated and popular kitchen with people always around drumming and singing and enjoying themselves (but also available to help). At the 2012 Gathering, however, they set up toward the outskirts of the Gathering, with winding trails and steep terrain surrounding them and the several dirty kids camps around them. Their assets (the cleanest water around, they said, because they had tapped the spring furthest up the mountain) and their challenges (their distance from "downtown" and the unwanted presence of alcohol resulting from their proximity to several dirty kids camps) were very different this year, at least in part due to their spatial location.

Another kitchen at the 2012 National Gathering experienced a similar surprise, albeit a more positive one. Camp Knothing is a newer, younger kitchen. They'd come to the 2012 Gathering without even intending to serve food; they were only going to serve coffee. However, the kitchen ended up very centrally located near the T, a major intersection of the Gathering where two main trails met and very near the main meadow. As Teddy told me,

> They've got this great central location right at the T, and so they got a lot of kick downs, and got them early. You know, everybody sharing the little that they had, and then they could combine things and make something delicious. Even the pots they use have been given to them because they didn't come planning to cook. But now they're a full kitchen, they're serving main circle, and people are loving what they do.

One of the ways that space becomes organized at a Gathering is through what I'll call participatory signage—individuals participate in the organization of space by hanging signs and banners that mark directions (to particular kitchens, water sources, shitters, and all sorts of other things) or indicate norms regarding the use of space (see Figures 3.3–3.5). Anyone can hang a sign, and lots of different Gathering participants (including children and Forest Service rangers) do; these signs help create a temporarily organized space, a material and physical community in the woods.

Figure 3.3: "Please Keep Use of Alcohol and Cell Phones in the Parking Lot." *Source:* Chelsea Schelly.

Figure 3.4: Pointing the way to Montana Mud. *Source:* Chelsea Schelly.

At the Tennessee Gathering, Dave and I spent one afternoon helping to hang thick pink and yellow ribbon, the Rainbow equivalent of caution tape, along the side of a trail with a very steep hill just off it. It was early in the Gathering, but someone had already fallen down the hill in the dark (my friend Sherlock, introduced in Chapter 2, who luckily didn't get hurt). Hearing about it the next day, a group of people decided to do something. They found some ribbon and tied it around trees, creating a sort of ribbon railing to warn people at each point the trail curved. This is the way that most things get done at a Rainbow Gathering: because people spontaneously decide to do them and make them happen.

This is not intended to shirk the importance of the handful of knowledgeable, involved folks who know the world and culture of Rainbow well and actively work to establish and maintain its spatial structure. Sometimes called elders, focalizers, or facilitators, these people take an active organizational role in making the Gathering happen, are aware of the needs and habits of Rainbow land, and help to shape its spatial structure. The norms of Rainbow (such as limiting alcohol use to the parking lots and A-camp) also contribute to the patterned spatial organization of Rainbow. Yet the spontaneous, ever-evolving, and participatory

Figure 3.5: "Please keep your pet well feed [*sic*], on a leash, out of the kitchen, dinner circles, and fights." *Source: Chelsea Schelly.*

ways of space-making, in which every gatherer is a potential participant in the meaningful creation of space and the shared understandings assigned to spatial organization, contribute in important ways to the social world of a Gathering.

Spatial Tension at the 2012 Rainbow Gathering

The 2012 Gathering demonstrated some of the tensions that have arisen in recent years between louder and rowdier dirty kids and the older, more peaceful (and non-drinking) hippies. At this Gathering, there were essentially three major divisions of space: A-camp in and near the parking lot on the Forest Service road at the bottom of a hillside slope; dirty kids corner with some drinking and rougher, rowdier energy at one end of the main trail; and the quieter side of the T where most of the older hippies camped.[15] (See Figure 3.6.)

While many of the kitchens that served the main circle dinner meal were more centrally located, the dirty kids kitchens carted meals for miles to serve food at main circle. Arguably, this was only possible for them because of the multitude of young and able bodies on hand at each kitchen to help lend a hand. Furthermore, this structural disadvantage resulted in both drawbacks and surprising boons: while the dirty kids kitchens were sometimes the last to show up to serve at the main circle meal and some elders and hungry gatherers grumbled about their lack of punctuality, they were also praised by some groups of elders for their determined efforts to consistently serve at the communal dinner despite the hard physical work required to traverse the distance while carrying heavy loads to get there.

Given the spatial organization of the Gathering, there were also multiple points to enter Rainbow land, and each trail off the parking lot had its own "front gate." One of these front gates—the first that newly arriving gatherers would drive past during the official week of the Gathering—was operated by

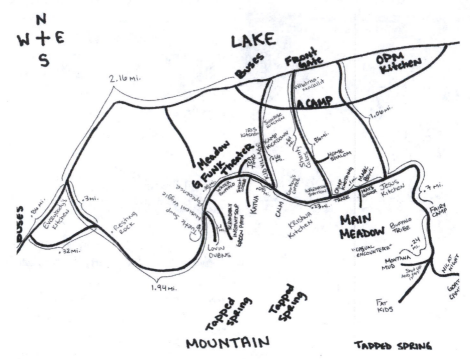

Figure 3.6: A map of the 2012 National Gathering. Distance estimates made using a pedometer. All errors and omissions are the author's responsibility. *Source:* Chelsea Schelly.

folks from a parking lot kitchen, some of whom completely disregarded the noncommercial spirit of the Gathering by asking people coming in for spare change. At another front gate you were greeted by several drunks sitting on the back end of a pickup parked right next to the main trail. Two miles down the road there were two more entries, one called "not front gate" and another called "not front gate again," where you were greeted by older Rainbow Family gatherers acting as a more peaceful, quiet, and loving front gate crew. Given these multiple entrances, it was possible to enter the Gathering without ever walking through A-camp. By avoiding A-camp, gatherers could spend the entire Gathering with either the spiritually oriented and peaceful hippies. Or gatherers could stay at the side of the Gathering with the louder and rowdier dirty kids and so completely avoid the other group. The tension between the two groups was clear in the spatial pattern that arose organically through the actions and decisions of hundreds, even thousands, of folks.

Dismantling a Temporary Metropolis:
Clean-Up Crew and the Leave-No-Trace Ethic

July 4 is the big event at a National Rainbow Gathering. It is the climax of attendance, energy, and use of the physical space that has become like a city in the woods. The Gathering officially lasts only a few days after July 4 (until July 7). By July 8 both the energy and the organization of the Gathering begin to noticeably shift, "when the mood of the gathering suddenly goes from peace and love and bliss to the party's over, get to work on cleanup or get out."[16] Many people go back home, some to their day jobs and other summertime activities, while others prepare for the massive work ahead in cleaning up the Rainbow Gathering site.

Since the very beginning, environmental responsibility and a leave-no-trace land-use ethic have been important parts of Rainbow Gathering culture. Every year, hundreds of people work to make sure that no trash is left behind, that every cigarette butt is picked up, that every fit pit, compost hole, and shitter is properly filled in and "disappeared," that every kitchen and campsite is completely dismantled and naturalized, and that every trampled meadow or newly made trail is appropriately reseeded.

Many kitchens leave before clean up begins, and kitchens that are planning to stay start to move into more centralized locations. In Tennessee, Fat Kids kitchen began moving to a more centralized space, where Jesus Kitchen had been, on July 6. Montana Mud, another kitchen that had been at the far end of the Gathering, also moved into a more central location. By July 8 there were plans to move yet again in order to consolidate kitchens around one main water line.

Water is one of the first considerations when it comes time to clean up. Miles of water line are run throughout the Gathering space, and as people begin to leave it becomes necessary to take up some of that line, give it back to the people who brought it with them, and consolidate resources and space so that the people who stay are centralized around one remaining water source. At the Tennessee Gathering, this meant that as early as July 8 the "clean-up crew" council decided to focus on dealing with the dirty kids side of the T first—meaning moving and "disappearing" all the kitchens, getting rid of all the trash, and completely naturalizing that area—and then consolidating the clean-up crew around a central location near the old "downtown."

The leave-no-trace ethic is an integral part of the participatory culture of Rainbow Gatherings (see Figure 3.7). Clean-up requires the active participation of many individuals who stay behind to help. Many participants in clean-up crew

Figure 3.7: Expression of the participatory, leave-no-trace ethic. *Source:* Chelsea Schelly.

are full-time travelers; as early as July 8 there is a noticeable shift in the population of gatherers still in the woods. Returning a natural area used by thousands of people to its original state takes weeks and involves multiple changes in the organization of space. The reorganization of the physical space during clean-up also changes the energy of the Gathering, in many ways intentionally. People are more likely to ask you to help pick up trash or carry a trash bag down to the parking lot if you're headed that way. One sister told me that one of the first things the clean-up crew does is get rid of "bliss pits" at the kitchens, to "change the vibe, you know. We're done hanging out, now it's time to help out or go home."

Negotiated Order and Patterned Anarchy

While every Gathering takes place at a different site, a similar spatial pattern emerges every year, within the context and confines of the specific location. Each Gathering is organized by a similar structural pattern (with different things located the same way, relative to one another), yet this organization emerges without direct leadership or formal organization of any kind. It develops through real-time interactions and negotiations between individual people working together to create this temporary metropolis in the woods.

The spatial organization of a Rainbow Gathering is organic and ever-evolving. Organization here is indeed a process,[17] or really a series of processes. It requires active participation by those who temporarily dwell in this unique social world and is demonstrated by the map hung at Information, which is never to scale and always changing as individuals add new kitchens, rest stops, and activity centers. Yet spatial organization is indeed patterned, taking similar form every year, with kitchens located and spaced similarly, with a centrally located meadow and a parking lot full of drunks, and with certain forms and functions, like water for drinking and bathing and spaces for buses and children, always present.

Participation in the processes of establishing spatial organization through participatory signage or through the interactions necessary to negotiate the use of space—interactions that are guided by an emphasis on love, peace, and respect—helps contribute to the positive emotional energy and collective culture of a Gathering. The space of a Gathering—the miles of trails through the National Forest that develop into a village in the woods—contributes to the energy of a Gathering in another important way. People can walk multiple miles every day to visit kitchens, help with supply runs, gather firewood, do other necessary tasks, or join in enjoyable daily activities. Sociologists often struggle to remember that the people they study are real humans with real bodies, but some—like Hans Joas—explicitly discuss how social action and interaction originate with corporality, with real bodies doing bodily things like making facial expressions and exercising through physical movement.[18] The physical exercise that is inherent in participation of any kind at a Gathering creates its own material energy, as individuals experience the rush of endorphins resulting from the exertion of physical energy in ways that they may not experience in any other space and time during the year. The very bodily yet simple experience of walking, wandering, and using physical energy in the natural world creates a physical, bodily response—an endorphin rush or energy high—that likely facilitates and contributes to the other types of physical and energetic highs created by the structure, culture, and experiences within the social world of a Rainbow Gathering.

The organization of Rainbow, although it is spatially and temporally patterned, requires active participation and allows for spontaneous leadership. It is what sociologist Anselm Strauss calls a *negotiated order*.[19] The concept of negotiated order involves "recognition of the intrinsically situational character of rules, which exist only in the perpetually renewed consensus of one situation after another."[20] Negotiated order emerges through the active participation and interaction of individuals.

Further, it is a temporary and fluid order. New water lines, camps, and kitchens enter the scene every day and then leave it just days or weeks later. The physical organization of a Gathering is fleeting. The form and energy of these temporary and nomadic events take shape only to disappear and reemerge again elsewhere. The spontaneous and participatory nature of the organic yet patterned physical organization of space at a Rainbow Gathering contributes to the culture and vibe of the Gathering itself. This is indeed the very point: to demonstrate the potential of active participation and the ability of human beings to contribute to the forming of their own worlds when they are free to do and be as they please.

CHAPTER 4

THE FREE WORLD OF RAINBOW

FOOD AND OTHER MATERIAL STUFF

Early in the 2012 Gathering, Dave and I ran into an old friend, Jackson, who invited us to the kitchen he was camped with and volunteering for (in Rainbow terminology, he was on the kitchen's "crew"). There I sat in on a kitchen council of one of the earliest kitchens to arrive that year. Gathered inside a tepee, a dozen or so people passed around a pipe filled with marijuana while a man called Lazy talked about the kitchen's organization and needs. A shirtless man in denim overalls perhaps in his early thirties, Lazy is clearly an authority at this kitchen. He has many of the qualities of a charismatic leader. Sociologist Max Weber thought that charismatic leadership was a particular form of leadership that appealed to people's affectual side—it is leadership that lures people's emotions, where people come to believe in a leader as a person and not just as a set of commitments or actions.[1] Talkative and articulate, confident and friendly, Lazy looks you right in the eye when he's speaking to you and knows just how to phrase things to evoke your most positive emotions (for example, by using the word "Family" a lot).

In this meeting, Lazy tells everyone how appreciative he is of their hard work so far and talks about some of the main aspects of the kitchen. The water system is set up and working well; he and another kitchen volunteer both had separate conversations with the Forest Service rangers that day about their filtration system, and both the rangers and the kitchen crew were pleased with it. He talked about the organization of their space and how they still needed to finish their serving station (called a "bliss rail"), construct the ovens, and mark the trail to the shitter. He told everyone that the area around the tepee, which was set up on a small hill just above the kitchen space, was intended to be and should be respected as family-friendly space—meaning that vulgar language should be kept to a minimum and that interaction with children should be expected, although it did not imply a need to restrict the use of marijuana in that space. He said he was working on creating a comprehensive wish list; these lists are hung in clear view in every kitchen so that other gatherers knew each kitchen's needs and could possibly help "manifest" the wished-for items. During the meeting, no one else had anything to say, and no specific tasks or roles were allocated. But by the next day, all the jobs discussed in that meeting were done.

Kitchens at the Gathering often work like this, with a charismatic leader or two (sometimes called "kitchen ogres"[2]) to help enroll volunteers and keep everyone apprised of the tasks that need accomplished. Usually, this person or these people are male, and their "right to leadership was granted by the behavior of all who came into the kitchen." Describing a well-liked Kid Village focalizer, Butterfly Bill writes, "People followed him willingly because they had already had good experiences in his kitchen and anticipated success if they did things according to his instructions." Butterfly Bill goes on to explain kitchen leadership in this way:

> Every kitchen had its lords, and when you were within the confines of their fiefdoms, you were not subject to any of its laws that had sanctions, but you were expected to respect its customs. A common way of rebuffing someone who was complaining was to say, "You don't like it? Go to another kitchen." And the real possibility that you could find another kingdom with customs more to your liking prevented there being any mutinies or rebellions. . . . Every kitchen had its own personality.[3]

Some people are crew with the same the kitchen every year, but nothing's set in stone. The free-form style of organization that characterizes these kitchens and food provision is consistent with the other material systems of the Gathering: food, water, sanitation, and medical care are all provided in an organic, nonhierarchical, participatory, and ever-evolving way. And there's always enough.

This chapter examines how the material world of a Rainbow Gathering is constructed, maintained, and organized. It focuses on how the particular forms of material organization at a Gathering—the freely provided sustenance that can only be successfully supplied through the hard physical work and active participation of many gatherers—contribute to and reinforce the cultural systems of a Gathering. The material systems that support life at a Gathering are freely available to all, but they require active participation and individual engagement. Individuals are rewarded for the efforts made to support and maintain the material organization of a Gathering tangibly and immediately; participation in the material organization of life is sustained by and helps to sustain Rainbow Gathering culture. Both the material and the culture systems of a Rainbow Gathering prioritize openness, connectivity, communal provision, and a collective spirit.

Kitchens: Meeting Material Needs through Participatory Provisioning

Kitchens serve a primary role at Rainbow Gatherings. Much of the voluntary participation that makes Gatherings possible comes from the individuals who put their energy into helping kitchens. Kitchens vary in size, style, and standards of sanitation. Yet they almost always include the same core components.

Kitchens cook food in large stainless-steel pots, on long metal sheets or atop grates over large fire pits, and in earthen ovens constructed out of mud and rocks, often with a metal barrel in the middle (see Figure 4.1). Food supplies come from several sources. They are brought in by people planning to associate with a kitchen, are "kicked down" by other attendees to the kitchens, and are purchased by Main Supply, which is funded by the Magic Hat. Food is served on a "bliss rail"—branches lashed together and connected to trees to create a countertop. A kitchen volunteer serves the food from the bliss rail—so a real, live, smiling human is there to fill your cup or bowl and often share a short but kind greeting or, if necessary, corrective instruction (such as reminding you to hold your bowl below the rim of the serving bowl, a measure intended to promote sanitation, or reminding you that no seconds are allowed until everyone has been served a first serving). Gatherers are served in their own individual bowl, or "bliss ware," which they carry with them at all times so that they can eat whenever a kitchen is serving (which can be absolutely any time of the day or night). Often, waiting for food requires standing in line with many others who have come in response to the call or the smells. Yet waiting in line is always another opportunity to meet a stranger, share in a hug, or listen to the music of a nearby minstrel who

Figure 4.1: Rainbow brother Skip standing next to earthen ovens at Lovin' Ovens kitchen, 2004 National Gathering. *Source:* Brother One Feather. Used with permission.

has stopped to play for those waiting to eat. Water and sometimes coffee or tea, depending on the kitchen, are also available on the bliss rail.

Kitchens make food at all different times of the night and day—pancakes in the evening, popcorn coated in nutritional yeast or marijuana-infused butter in the middle of the night, coffee all day. Walking down a trail or sitting at your camp, you'll hear occasional calls of "Free food in the woods!" The actual words are often indiscernible, but it is an indication to walk that way if you're hungry.

Funds from the Magic Hat are used to buy supplies for the kitchens—large quantities of simple and durable food like rice, beans, flour, onions, garlic, squash, and so on. Only kitchens that serve food at main circle and Kid Village have access to food through Main Supply. Other kitchens rely on their own resources (including pooled food stamps) and "kick-downs" (donations of food and other supplies from other gatherers).

Montana Mud has been a coffee kitchen (serving "mud") since the mid-1980s. Some of the people who help run this kitchen once told me that they have a particular reputation: it's a place where heroin or opiate addicts can go to get clean. They are loud and rowdy, serving coffee twenty-four hours a day during the official week of the Gathering. They also serve food at main circle. The main facilitator of the kitchen has been volunteering in this capacity for eight years now; an elder who was ready to transition out of the facilitating role passed on the position to him.

Many of the people who volunteer on this kitchen crew are indeed from Montana. This is partially what is meant by "a Gathering of the tribes"—people from different regions of the country organize kitchens and then come together so that multiple kitchens from various regions are all together in the woods serving one another and everyone else who comes to gather. Montana Mud is from Montana; Katuah kitchen is from the Appalachia region; folks from Michigan organize Turtle Soup; friends from New York started Camp Knothing. As Teddy told me, "A lot of these kitchens have been doing this for years, and some of them know each other well. It really is like a Gathering of the tribes."

Tea Time is a kitchen that exclusively serves tea and has at every National Gathering since the 1980s. One of the main facilitators for Tea Time has been actively involved since 1992. He told me that most of the people helping out at Tea Time know each other from past Gatherings and in their Babylonian lives, but that's not the case for everybody. They usually have a large crew of volunteers, up to seventy people helping to brew and serve multiple kinds of tea twenty-four hours a day. While they do not serve food, they do provide food for their crew, serving breakfast and dinner to those who help run the kitchen.

When I went to visit Tea Time at the 2012 Gathering, three "tea fairies"—young, attractive women wearing costume wings while serving tea—greeted me. They asked me to ring the bell hung next to the bliss rail for service. Then one of them told me the multiple kinds of tea that they had to serve (including black teas, green teas, chamomile tea, and sassafras tea) while the other reached for my cup, waited for my choice, and served me.

As I walked away, they cheerily yelled, "Don't forget, it's a two-cup minimum! Come back anytime; just don't forget to ring the bell!" From a distance, I could still hear occasional chants of "What time is it? Tea time!"

Other Systems of Provision: Water, Sanitation, and Waste

Essential for life, clean drinking water is certainly essential for the thousands of people who gather every summer for the National Rainbow Gathering. The

Figure 4.2: The "water buffalo" and filtration system at Fat Kids kitchen, 2012 National Gathering. Their water tasted slightly sweet because they use an old Mountain Dew syrup canister. *Source:* Chelsea Schelly.

availability of water is a key component of choosing a site for each Gathering, and elaborate systems of PVC piping and water filtration units ensure that everyone has access to clean drinking water. Every kitchen usually has filtered water available, and sometimes water stations are set up along the trail so that people can drink and fill up their water bottles without having to find a kitchen (see Figures 4.2–4.4).

Crum, a broad, shirtless man with long curly hair, told me about his role in helping four different kitchens get clean water at the 2012 Gathering and how those involved in organizing the water system made it happen. We talked while standing next to a filtration system he was attempting to install high up the rocky, hilly terrain, with trails of black water pipe winding through the trees to several kitchens all around us.

> We sort of knew that these kitchens would be over here, and the meadow was
> kinda central, and that we'd have to take care of the other end too. So three of
> us, we talked about it, and split up the work. I probably have five miles of piping
> running through the woods back here. I climbed up to the top and got the tap

Figures 4.3 and 4.4: Miles and miles of water lines are run throughout the woods, 2012 National Gathering. Can you find the water lines in these photos? *Source: Chelsea Schelly.*

going—it's in a creek just a short way down from the source spring—and then had a bunch of kids helping to walk the lines through the woods. I showed up with about two miles of pipe, and we all knew that we'd try to get both ends running all the way to the meadow, but that's all based on what supplies show up, and how much.

As we were chatting, a young man wearing all black came up to join us, and he asked Crum about drinking "live" (unfiltered) water. "As far as I know," Crum said, "I'm the only person that's been all the way up to the source. And I trust it. Don't you ever serve that in your kitchens, always boil or filter your water. But you can be the judge for your own body, and for me, I've been drinking it for two weeks. Comes through a real steep section, not many animals living up there to shit in this water."

Crum and the few other folks who took a facilitating role in providing the water supply would spend part of every day at the Gathering adding new lines as more people and supplies arrived. Dozens of other voluntary participants would clean and change filters, refill large water containers, and haul water through the woods to ensure that kitchens had clean water for all those who stopped. Making filtered drinking water available to all who gather requires hard work, active participation, and knowledge of the natural world. Those who participate are supported by a culture that rewards their efforts both tangibly and energetically.

Another use of water is washing, both dishes and bodies. Each kitchen has a dishwashing station for attendees to wash their bliss ware. The standard dishwashing station at a Rainbow Gathering involves three five-gallon buckets, each with varying levels of soap and/or bleach for cleaning, rinsing, and sanitizing dishes. Sometimes these are simply sitting on the ground; other times they are up on counters made out of tree limbs.

From bathing to bowel movements, much of what is considered "backstage"[4] in Babylon—privately away from the realities, expectations, and pressures of social performance—happens publicly at a Gathering. Some Gathering sites have a swimming hole, a natural water source large enough for bathing or at least rinsing. Kitchens and camps also set up solar showers, made from black water containers for heating the water with the power of the sun and a hose fixture hanging from the bottom; showers are especially prevalent in cooler locations like the National Gathering that took place high in the mountains of northeastern California. One shower set up at the Tennessee Gathering had two sides to it, with two long pieces of PVC piping hung from trees and a tarp hung vertically in between them. Someone who put the shower up at the kitchen told me, "One side's the 'give a shit' side, one side's the 'don't give a shit' side, since only one provides privacy. I'd prefer not to have the tarp there, for aesthetic reasons, but a lot of people like having the privacy; so the 'don't give a shit' side is usually available, and I guess that's nice."

Shitters are always located near (but not too near[5]) kitchens. While they vary significantly in privacy and comfort, they always involve certain structures and principles: a deep and long trench, a bucket (often an old coffee can) with toilet paper, and a bucket of lime or ash from the fires or lime to cover your waste. Some kitchens build structures with toilet seats on them, so that these trench shitters seem not much different than an outdoor outhouse. Others require squatting over the trench. Some have privacy curtains and homemade signs indicating occupation or vacancy, while others do not. Most gatherers quickly figure out which kitchens have the "best shitters" and visit that kitchen for their bodily needs more frequently.

Hauling supplies and gear down miles of trail involves spontaneous forms of human organization, collective involvement, and often some makeshift equipment. Every day, food must be brought from Main Supply in the parking lot up to each kitchen, and then prepared food must travel from each kitchen to main circle. Most kitchens have carts of some kind for hauling food and other kitchen equipment; these carts are usually moved by at least two people, one pushing, one pulling. People sometimes use logs to carry large loads by tying things to it and having two people carry, each with one end on their shoulder. There is flexibility to this participation; people wandering the trails are often asked to help with loads, and people often stop to offer.

The work required to construct, maintain, and pack out a Gathering happens in an organic, spontaneous way. Although some people who regularly help out with one particular kitchen may develop habits or routines, there are new people who plug in every year, and the people who help to make kitchens successful face a new set of opportunities and requirements in every day and each new moment. Those who get up early may start the fire and the coffee or tea every day; someone who just arrived might help carry multiple loads of firewood; several people might help plan and prepare the main circle meal, and it may be a different set of folks every night. A regular with one kitchen told me, "The kitchen is a really organic space. It's about giving everything up and just knowing that every thing will get taken care of. I love to see how that manifests every year, and really, that's kind of the point, to give people a space to open up and to trust."

Rainbow Technology: Material Systems That Require Active Participation

Lazy once told me, "You know, there are supposedly 30,000 people in America who are Rainbow Family. There are only about 200 who are really involved and know what needs to get done. But none of it really would get done without all the kids out here helping." It is often the younger folks who are (or at least appear to be) permanent travelers, street kids, homeless folks, and others who may be considered "unproductive" members of mainstream society (Babylon) who work the hardest, carrying food and water and piping and supplies up and down miles of trail to ensure that people can freely eat, drink, and celebrate. Arguably, they actively participate without monetary reward because Gathering culture trusts their knowledge, appreciates their efforts, and rewards their actions through a heightened sense of collective connectivity.

All of the work necessary to freely provide food, water, sanitation, and health care to all those who gather occurs through voluntary participation. The material systems of a Gathering are inherently participatory, requiring active, physical involvement. Some of the people who work as crew for a particular kitchen know each other, while others have just met. Some people spend their days helping with one kitchen exclusively; some people focus their energies entirely on medical care (through CALM), water crew, shitter-digging crew, or facilitating at the information booth; others assist wherever they happen to be; and some gatherers don't help at all. Yet it is through freely provided and accessible opportunities that gatherers participate in the material world of a Gathering and enjoy the fruits of their efforts. Relatively conventional and routine activities like eating, dishwashing, and defecating take on new meaning in this unique social world as they become emotively connected to the communal experience.[6]

Some Norms of Material Practice

The material systems that support life at a Rainbow Gathering involve unique forms of low-tech provisioning that require active engagement and participation. These unique material systems involve a correspondingly unique set of cultural norms regarding practice. Because of the free supply of both food and water, carrying around the necessary equipment—a bowl, an eating utensil, and a bottle for water—is standard practice at a Gathering. Most people have their bliss ware (often called simply "bliss") with them at all times, attached to their belts or in a backpack, so that they can always stop to eat at a kitchen when some good smelling grub is being served. If you show up without bliss, a kitchen is sure to have extra—often an emptied plastic container or the cut-off bottom half of a plastic jug—for anyone who asks. In addition to having your own eating utensils, you are expected to have a means of carrying water or holding other beverages such as coffee and tea.

Carrying your bliss with you at all times is not the only norm or standard practice—calling them rules would be inaccurate—related to the material systems unique to this social world. There are other norms related to keeping the Gathering sanitary and gatherers healthy. When you are served, you are expected to hold your bliss below the serving pot so that no food touches your bowl and then falls back in the large communal pot. When you get water or ask for a drink from someone else's water, you are expected not to touch the rim of your bottle or your lips to the spout or container. These norms are enforced by the Rainbow phrase, "Don't touch your thing to the thing," modified by dirty kids kitchens to "Don't touch your shit to the shit."

In reference to another kind of shit, there are certain norms regarding the use of the shitters. Gatherers are expected to use communal shitters exclusively (as opposed to digging your own personal hole or defecating anywhere else) because communal and collective feces is easier to deal with in terms of sanitation and health than feces spread all over the place. After using a communal latrine, waste should always be covered with ash or lime. Because there are so many dogs at a Gathering, you may also be asked to bury or cover your dog's waste. As Rap 107 states: "Shit-Flies-Food-You: Break the connection!" Gatherers conscientiously adopt norms of practice that make it possible to safely live with communal systems of provision based on sharing food, water, spaces for bathing, and spaces for depositing waste. These freely shared systems and the norms of practice that shape and support them both contribute to the energetically charged communal Gathering experience.

Synergistic Relationships between Material and Cultural Systems

These few norms regarding food, water, and waste are arguably about sanitation:[7] they are requests made by the Family to the Family in order to keep the Family safe and healthy. Yet these norms—being served by a volunteer rather than serving yourself, preparing food and eating collectively, using the collective camp fires, boiling or filtering all water served to others, and following poop protocol—as well as the physical systems themselves (such as kitchens that serve communal meals and communally used latrines) contribute to and reinforce the culture of a Gathering. These material systems and the practices surrounding them help focus each individual on collectivity, interdependence, and connection. The qualities of these material systems—free and open to all, communally shared, and requiring participation—contribute to the unique social experience of a Gathering.

The material systems that support life at a Rainbow Gathering through communal provision of food, water, sanitary facilities, hygiene, and health care are all provided freely and are only made possible through the participation of many different people in the construction, establishment, maintenance, support, and then dismantling of these systems. These temporary material systems enroll gatherers in a particular set of bodily practices that are more communal, collective, and participatory than those found in mainstream American life.

When you are hungry at a Gathering, you must—along with dozens or hundreds of other gatherers—find a kitchen serving food. Because of all the work involved in providing free food to all those who gather, you may be asked to help haul food supplies to a kitchen or to collect firewood or wash dishes for the kitchen after you've eaten. When you are thirsty, you must find and use a water buffalo publicly available at a kitchen or along the trail. While you may not actually relieve your bowels in the physical presence of another gatherer, it's also possible that you may, and it's certainly likely that someone else will be waiting their turn. If you want to bathe, you will use a communal swimming hole or shared shower system. If you need medical help for anything from poison ivy, a wound that needs bandaged, or dehydration to the symptoms of a bad acid trip or opiate withdrawal, you will walk to CALM where volunteers freely provide all the information and supplies that they have available to them. The culture of a Rainbow Gathering emphasizes collectivity, connection, and interdependence, creating a sense of self that is deeply intertwined with the feelings of collective solidarity.[8] The material systems of a Rainbow Gathering contribute to and reinforce this culture; the free, open, and participatory material systems contribute to the sense of collective effervescence experienced by gatherers.

Material and technological systems, from buildings[9] to systems of food provision, shape cultural systems. One of the ways that material systems influence cultural systems is by enrolling the body in different techniques, ways of using the body, actions that involve interaction with the physical world.[10] As Marcel Mauss proclaims, "we are everywhere faced with physio-psycho-sociological assemblages of series of action."[11]

In other words, we learn how to physically interact with the material systems we use. Material systems shape our actions and interactions. Hygiene and food consumption and myriad other forms of interaction with the material world involve learned patterns of bodily practice, sometimes called *techniques* in sociology.[12] These techniques of the body are learned through social interaction, and they come to shape what we expect from our social interactions as well as our expectations of and reactions to the organization of the world around us. The ways we eat, drink, deal with our own waste, and even brush our teeth are culturally learned and culturally mediated practices.

Further, the learned system of actions and interactions that correspond with using material systems become habits, which engrain and reinforce culture. Techniques of the body—patterns of bodily practice that arise through interactions with both the social and material world—shape the organization of our social world, our interactions within it, and our conceptions of normal or accepted organization and practice. Through practices of the actual physical body, material systems shape cultural systems. Bodily actions and interactions mediate between material systems and cultural systems. Our interactions with the material world and with one another as humans utilizing material systems teach us about cultural expectations regarding how we ought to interact with one another and with the world around us. There is, as Mauss describes it, a "concourse of the body and moral or intellectual symbols"[13] that takes place through our interactions with the physical world.

The material systems of a Rainbow Gathering involve bodily practices that are collective, participatory, and open to all. Food is provided freely and prepared and eaten collectively. Water, sanitation, hygiene, and health care also involve open, communal, participatory action and interaction. The bodily practices involved in engaging and interacting with the material systems of a Rainbow Gathering connect the material and the cultural, and the organization of the material world works to reinforce the collective experiences of Rainbow Gathering culture.

CHAPTER 5
RAINBOW SPEAK

LANGUAGE AND COMMUNICATION

Driving into a Rainbow Gathering, the first thing you will probably hear is "Welcome home!" You will hear this phrase again and again as you walk through the parking lot, pass the front gate, carry your gear into the woods to find a camp spot, and throughout your time at a Gathering. After hearing it over and over, you will likely find yourself saying it to others who seem to have just arrived. For the Rainbow Family of the Living Light, these words carry great significance because when they gather, they are home. For veterans who returned home from the unpopular war in Vietnam, veterans of wars since, and all those who feel separate from or ostracized by mainstream American society, "that simple phrase carries important meaning," according to a longtime Rainbow participant who calls himself Roadrunner, who is a Vietnam veteran.[1]

The Rainbow Family has many unique words and phrases within their vocabulary.[2] Much of the vocabulary particular to this social world—like "Welcome home"—matches and helps contribute to the positive emotional energy of this ritual event. In addition to "Welcome home," you will hear the words "Lovin' you" from smiling strangers you pass on the trail and "We love you!" shouted out through the darkness by gatherers at night. Strangers will call you brother or sister or mama or family as they pass you on the trail and say hello. These "little ceremonies of greeting and farewell"[3] set Rainbow Gatherings apart as a unique social world. The words, phrases, and ways of communicating that enter the ritual of speech exchange[4] at a Gathering shape the ways participants interact with one another and experience life in this temporary world. The unique language of this social world contributes to the sense of collectivity and connection, the heightened sense of collective effervescence, experienced by many of those who gather.

The Vocabulary of Connection

Fitting for those who see themselves as one spiritual Family,[5] Rainbow gatherers address one another as brother, sister, or mama. "Hello, brother," "Good afternoon, sister," and "Lovin' you, mama" are examples of fairly common greetings among strangers. You hear the word "Family" a lot at the Gathering; "Lovin' you, Family" is a typical way to say hello or goodbye to any group of people.

Just as the Gathering is "home" and the people there are "Family," spaces and tools take on familiar domestic terms. Gatherers sometimes refer to kitchens as their "house." "Someone in our house" means "someone in the kitchen." Jackson once told me, "We've got a broom up at the house you can use," by which he meant there's a rake at the kitchen that I could borrow (to create a flat spot free of rocks and branches to pitch a tent). Even forms of spatial organization can take on familiar terms, like calling the central and most densely populated area of the Gathering "downtown."

Sharing food[6] and other forms of sustenance freely is an important part of the culture and value system of the Rainbow Family, and several unique vocabulary words are related to these provisions. Food, and the many types of "bliss" that it involves, brings gatherers together as participants in a unique social world that prioritizes sharing, equality, and connectivity. The bowl, plate, or other things carried individually to hold food are called "bliss" or "bliss ware." Someone on a kitchen crew might yell out, "Bliss! Who needs some bliss!" before a meal and hand out extra plastic containers or bowls for those who need them. The place where food is served at a kitchen is called a "bliss rail." Fire pits for hanging around (as opposed to cooking over) are often called "bliss pits" (or, if they are large and made specifically for hosting drum circles and the dancing that sometimes accompanies the drumming, they are occasionally referred to as "boogie pits").

There are particular words for various roles people play within the Rainbow Family, such as elder, kitchen ogre, drainbow, and bliss ninny. Suborganizations unique to this social world also have their own names. A-campers camp in A-camp; front gators help out at front gate. When a significant issue of violence or confrontation arises, people witnessing the event will yell "Shanti Sena!" and anyone who considers themselves a peacekeeper of the Gathering will come help resolve the issue through peaceful means.

Although misunderstandings can arise "during interaction between persons who come from groups with different ritual standards"[7]—like between gatherers and the Forest Service rangers that patrol the Gathering—the language of the Rainbow Family, particularly the many expressions of positivity and connection, are often used to address even potentially conflictual relationships. At the 2012 National Gathering, I was sitting on the side of a trail resting with Lazy and several other folks (what's called a "road block," where a cluster of Rainbow folks stop on the main trail for a break from wherever they were going and whatever they were doing) when rangers approached and began talking with Lazy about the water source and water filtration methods at the kitchen he helps organize. Lazy told the rangers that the water had been tested two months prior to their arrival, a month ago, and just last week when they arrived, to make sure they had the correct kinds of filters for the Gathering. He talked about how important it was to him to "keep the Family safe and healthy" and how he was doing it all "for the good of the entire Family." He told the rangers that he made sure the water was safe "even for our babies and pregnant mamas." He made steady eye contact with the rangers, and, without any tension at all, Lazy had seemingly enrolled the rangers in the trust-based, family-oriented values of the Gathering through the use of Rainbow language.

This language is sometimes even adopted by rangers themselves. At the 1988 National Gathering, access to the National Forest was temporarily blockaded by the National Forest Service. On the day the restriction was lifted, a ranger driving a Forest Service SUV announced through the speaker attached to the cab that the closure had been lifted, concluding with "and so on behalf of the Forest Service we say, 'Welcome Home.'"[8]

The Vocabulary of Separation

Many of the terms in Rainbow vernacular highlight the connectivity between those who attend Gatherings, bringing them together as Family at home. In contrast, some of the vocabulary unique to this social world helps to separate the Gathering from Babylon (itself a term of separation). This separation from mainstream society, in turn, further solidifies the collectivity of life at a Gathering.

For instance, "Rainbow names" are incredibly common. Most people don't introduce themselves as Joe, Jon, or Jack. Rather, they are Raven, Blackfoot, Kentucky, Karma, and all sorts of other things. Occasionally people will tell you both their "slave names" (those they use in Babylon) and their Rainbow names, but most of the time you only get the fanciful, chosen one. At Gatherings, I've met folks like Fisher, Hugger, Patches, Squirrel, Skittles, Spirit, Springer, Shipwreck, Turtle, and Tigger. I once heard a Rainbow elder tell a small group of people sitting around a kitchen, "You can't call yourself Raven or Hawk anything anymore, because there's already one. And there are bears of every color doing everything you can imagine, Red Bear and Blue Bear and Sitting Bear and Dancing Bear and Fucking Bear. And don't call yourself Sunshine or Butterfly, there's way too many of those." To this, a younger Rainbow brother responded, "Hey man, I've met a lot of beautiful Sunshines."

Even little kids adopt Rainbow names. I once heard a little boy correcting someone, saying defiantly, "Here, my name's not Levi, it's Little Hawk!" As a unique group of Gathering participants, Forest Service representatives sometimes adopt Rainbow language and I've even heard a Forest Service ranger get into the Rainbow name game. Approaching a grizzly looking man at the front gate that he seemed to be on friendly terms with, I've overheard a ranger ask, "Hey, you got a Rainbow name yet?" (Of course, the man did.) "Well, I was thinking of one for you, you know, what about Barko? 'Cause it's like Marco, but you got a good bark!" The ranger was clearly amused and the folks around the front gate—likely already drunk by the middle of the day—also laughed.

People call themselves all sorts of things, and Rainbow names have all sorts of spiritual, metaphorical, or personal significance for those who adopt them. I once had a first-timer tell me, "A man named Chief gave me my Rainbow name; he's, well, a Chief. He named me Raven. He said it's like a symbol of freedom, of reaching for freedom. And that's really what I've been doing here; it's like opening a process of freeing myself."

Rainbow names also contribute to the anonymity and the culture of freedom at a Gathering. Introducing yourself as Sunshine or Sparrow or Shipwreck is another indication that this social world is uniquely distinct and that what happens within this ephemeral ritual event is unlike what takes place in the profane world of Babylon. Rainbow names are chosen, a symbol of the freedom of expression at a Gathering.

Just as Rainbow names carry a symbolic significance, so too does the language around time at a Gathering. Watches (tools of Babylon) are called "babylo-meters" and time is tracked and referred to in a much looser fashion. "Good morning" is a typical greeting all throughout the day, from dawn until dusk. Things at night are said to take place at "dark thirty." Daily council meetings take place at "Rainbow noon," and the silence on July 4 is broken by the Om circle around Rainbow noon, with a parade of children entering the main meadow at some point when the sun is high in the sky.

This relationship to time and the vocabulary surrounding it seem to be shifting. Happenings like plant walks and yoga classes have been listed at exact times at recent Gatherings. Even the signs for main circle at the 2012 National Gathering indicated an exact time (6:00 p.m.), although the meal never takes place with such precision or consistency. The increasing presence of cell phones and greater range of phone service likely influence the use of time in this space where blatantly ignoring the time—as well as the day of the week or day of the month, for those who come to the Gathering without a specified departure date—was once actively encouraged by language such as "babylo-meter."

Other material objects also have names that mark them as unique. The large water containers (often 50- or 100-gallon tanks) that hold filtered water are called "water buffalos." The canisters full of tobacco that the Nic at Night crew carry around are not called canisters but "buskets." Sweets and treats like chocolate, cake, and candy bars are rare at a Gathering relative to sugar-powered Babylon, and they are lumped together in a category of their own called "zu zus." People sometimes barter with and for zu zus at trade circle, and sometimes kitchens have "zu zu movie nights."

The word "movie" has a unique meaning at a Rainbow Gathering. It translates, generally, as "activity." I once heard Lazy say to his kitchen crew, "If you're not involved in another movie, we need firewood!" One afternoon, Jackson told me, "We're gonna have another cake movie here tonight, at dark thirty"—meaning the kitchen was going to make and serve cake that evening after the sun went down.

Communication with and about law enforcement officers and Forest Service rangers also highlights the uniqueness of this social world. The words "six up" are used to indicate the presence of law enforcement, and there is a more recent modification of the term used for Forest Service resource managers ("seven up"). Some gatherers explain this distinction as "those with guns" and "those without guns." I once had a woman tell me, "If you can't tell whether it's six up or seven up, just look at the belt. The ones with guns have wider belts."

Whenever local law enforcement officers or the more frequently seen Forest Service rangers are driving through the parking lot or walking down the trail, these words are shouted out by gatherers, and these shouts follow the officers and rangers everywhere they go. Dozens of people shout out the call, and then the next group to see them does the same, letting everyone know where they are and which direction they're traveling at all times. At a Rainbow Gathering, no one should ever be surprised or caught off guard by the legal officials who come from outside to police the woods; this unique language allows the Family to help protect one another from potential legal troubles.

Rangers certainly come to notice and understand this language. One morning, a group of rangers came to visit Jackson's camp. When they were leaving, a ranger asked him, "Which one are we, six up or seven up?" When he told her "Seven up," she smiled, turned, and yelled "Seven up!" just like a gatherer would have before she continued walking down the trail. I once overheard a ranger say to her colleagues as they were conversing about the shouts following them down the trail, "You know, it's really kind of a good thing for us. It makes our jobs easier. This way, we don't have to see anything we don't want to see or deal with anything we don't want to deal with. I think it's nice."

However, some less experienced gatherers don't completely understand how this vocalized warning signal works at its best. The intention with the call is to have it follow the rangers as they walk so that people always know where they are and which direction they are walking. Sometimes, younger folks or first-timers just get really into shouting this phrase and do so anytime they hear anybody else do it. I once heard an elder scolding a younger man for yelling "Six up!" inappropriately. In the end, though, and in characteristic Rainbow fashion, love and appreciation trumped frustration: After an obviously frustrated attempt to explain how the signal should work, he added, "And thank you. Thank you for helping keep your Family safe!"

Ways of Communication

The organizational and form of governance at Rainbow Gatherings—where participants make decisions by consensus in open councils—also encourages a unique language around leadership and those that choose to take what would in mainstream society be referred to as leadership roles. Meetings are called "councils" (jokingly called "clown-sils" by those within the Family who are critical of consensus-based decision making). In council, people wait for their turn to hold a feather that is passed from person to person to share their "heart song"—basically whatever it is they'd like to share with all those present.

Instead of leaders, folks are referred to as focalizers and facilitators. Focalizers and facilitators participate in councils, help to keep things organized, and keep track of the organizational needs of the Gathering. Kitchens often have one or two people that act as facilitators for the kitchen, and they also have representatives or "crew"—consistent volunteers who help pick up food from Main Supply, serve food at main circle, and participate in kitchen councils. Council as a term is used generally, but there are several different kinds of councils, from the daily council and the separate daily kitchen council to Shanti Sena (peacekeepers) council, clean-up council, banking council, spring council where the exact location of the annual Gathering is decided, and the annual "Vision Council" to select a region or state for the next year's Gathering.

The methods of communication at a Rainbow Gathering are also unique. While some are based on practicality, others are influenced by the broader values and cultural practices of the Family. Many of the focalizers and facilitators at a National Gathering communicate with one another using walkie-talkies; this is practical given the distances and lack of routine at a Gathering, since people can really be anywhere at any time. This system is used to communicate needs, crises, and other happenings. For instance, volunteers at Information use walkie-talkies to communicate with kitchens down the trail when six up is headed their way.

The presence of a walkie-talkie system is arguably the only exclusive form of communication at a Gathering. Most communication happens directly, openly, freely, and publicly. People look each other in the eye as common practice. Saying hello and sharing a smile with nearly everyone you pass is an integral part of Rainbow culture. People stop for casual, spontaneous conversation anywhere and everywhere—in a kitchen, in a meadow, on the side of the trail, sometimes even in the middle of the trail.

At the 2012 Gathering, several self-appointed mail carriers wandered the trails at all times of day and night, voluntarily providing other people the opportunity to write a letter and then attempting to deliver them. Given that anyone could write a letter to anyone, this system was used for all sorts of things, from the serious to the completely silly. Letters were sometimes addressed to kitchens, or specific people at specific kitchens, but sometimes they were addressed to "anyone who believes in the 2012 prophecies" or "some hot dready mama" (meaning a woman with dreadlocks, which are in abundance among the Rainbow Family). Throughout the day and into the evening, these voluntary mail carriers wan-

Figure 5.1: "How to shit: 1. Follow ribbons to slit-trench, 2. Shit only in trench. 3. Please wipe butt. 4. Cover shit and paper with ash, lime, soil. 5. WASH HANDS. 6. Feel great." *Source:* Chelsea Schelly.

dered from place to place, helping people communicate. Of course, signs made by anyone for anything also help communicate expected practices and values (see Figures 5.1–5.3).

Another Rainbow term is "Rainbow rumors"—of which there are many—and Rainbow rumors are one of the ways that people communicate at a Gathering. Some of the tales of violent occurrences in A-camp seem to be rumors (although

Figure 5.2: A sign on a car in the parking lot at the 2012 National Gathering. *Source:* Chelsea Schelly.

Figure 5.3: "Snakes like water and cool nights—This is their home, use respect and caution." *Source:* Chelsea Schelly.

fights certainly do happen there). There are always rumors about "doses" (drugs) and "dosers" (people who give them away for free)—when they're coming and where to find them and other tales—although there are usually at least a couple dosers with doses at every National Gathering. At the Tennessee Gathering, I heard a rumor, without any sense of its source or purpose but with absolute certainty of its falsity, that all the cars remaining in the parking lot were going to be towed on July 5. One of the Rainbow rumors that people quickly learn to avoid is that of cancellation. Sometimes, rumors spread in the spring that the National Gathering is not going to happen that summer, but it always does.

Rainbow rumors are one of the ways that people communicate at a Gathering— through the hyperbolized, the surreal, and sometimes the downright imaginary. "We find social relationships simplified, while myth and ritual are elaborated."[9] Perhaps this is because of the acceptance and even encouragement of the fantastical or because of the lack of official documentation and hierarchical communication. It may be at least partially explainable by the presence of mentally not-well folks at a Gathering or due to the inevitability of human misunderstandings. Some of the rumors may be simple playfulness, as people communicate for the sake of connection.[10] The abundance of Rainbow rumors is also at least partially cultural, as accepting the expression and possibility of any and every truth contributes to the openness, freedom, and connectivity experienced at a Gathering. Tales, Rainbow rumors, spread about almost anything and everything; the term and all the stories that get labeled with it are an important part of the freedom of expression that tends toward collective anarchy at a Rainbow Gathering.

One of the biggest changes in how humans communicate is, of course, the Internet. When Rainbow Gatherings started, people learned about the events through mailed invitations and telephone "light lines." While the light lines still exist, most people now get directions to the National Gathering online, and there are websites and Facebook groups full of Rainbow Family information (although none of it can be considered official). The Internet makes information regarding Rainbow Gatherings more accessible, and arguably more people attend for a larger diversity of reasons because of it. Rainbow Family participants also communicate with one another via the Internet, of course, and communications in cyberspace present another opportunity and challenge for practicing peaceful, respectful, and tolerant communication—supposed pillars of communication at a Gathering.

Open Communication in an Open Culture: Communication as Ritual Interaction

A unique and shared vocabulary is one of the indicators of a social world,[11] and the common language, words, and terms exclusive to Rainbow Gathering culture are a distinctive mark that set this unique and sacred social world apart from the profane[12] world of Babylon. Much of this language involves means of practical communication in this temporary social space. The unique ways of communicating operate as cues of togetherness. They are shaped by and in turn reinforce cultural values, and they are vehicles of connectivity among gatherers. They contribute to the uniqueness of the social world and the culture of openness and peacefulness. "Every person lives in a world of social encounters,"[13] and the unique vocabulary and forms of expression at a Rainbow Gathering generate social encounters that evoke consistently positive emotional reactions and feelings of connectivity as part of "the logic of the ritual game."[14]

Sociologist Georg Simmel used the term *sociability* to describe a form of social interaction in which the "aim is nothing but the success of the sociable moment."[15] Sociability is communication with no objective or outside motive; in sociability, "talk becomes its own purpose."[16] This describes a lot of the conversation that takes place at a Rainbow Gathering. In contrast to Babylon, where people often talk simply to give or receive instruction, strategize, or schmooze for the sake of some expected reward, people at Rainbow Gatherings talk for the sake of connection[17] and "even mundane sociality is associated with a pervasive stimulation of energy within and between individuals."[18]

Open, peaceful communication does not mean perfect communication. It takes work for those participating in Shanti Sena to speak and act peacefully in nonpeaceful situations. It takes work to communicate peacefully across potential power dynamics and conflicted relationships.[19] Consensus processes in councils are messy and time consuming and do not guarantee that everyone speaks respectfully, listens attentively, or participates with an open heart. Some of the openness in communication arguably encourages sexually predatory behavior, as men (and occasionally women) sometimes feel free to stare too deeply or communicate their sexual interests or desires too aggressively. Yet Rainbow Gatherings do provide a space where people can practice open communication and push the boundaries of communication. Butterfly Bill says that the value of a Rainbow Gathering lies "in the lessons it could teach, and the satisfaction you get from confronting problems and enduring."[20] These lessons are based on learning new and better ways of communicating with one another as well as new and better ways of interacting.

At a Gathering, the unique vocabulary and ways of communicating operate to connect people to one another. People experience a sense of collectivity because their language and practices of communication are exclusive to this social world. The words and phrases themselves work to heighten people's sense of connection. They are the language of family, the language of love. People openly make eye contact, say hello, and communicate with strangers. Signs and the mail carriers operate as public, communal forms of communication. People have the freedom to say anything and everything. These aspects of the interaction ritual at a Gathering contribute to the heightened connectivity among gatherers. The sense of collective effervescence that people experience at a Rainbow Gathering is in part developed through the words, forms of expression, and interactions that enter ritualized communication in this social world.

Chapter 6

The Free Life of Rainbow

Hugs and Other Ways to Touch

The cultural practices that take place within the social world of a Rainbow Gathering work to create and enhance a unique experience of open communication, active participation, and connected collectivity. Many nonverbal means of communicating and other physical, bodily practices also operate as ways of connecting with fellow gatherers at an emotional level. A woman named Mallory, who traveled from Ohio to attend the 2012 Gathering, described it this way: "This is a respite from the world where you walk by people on the street and they don't even say hello . . . where you think of every stranger as dangerous. Where every person fends for themselves. Here, we all fend for each other."[1] From hugs to helping to trading to collective yelling, there are multiple ways to connect with other gatherers through bodily action and interaction that work to heighten the collective energy of the event. These physical forms of connection and the cultural norms shaping nonverbal forms of communication—from eye contact and hugs to nakedness and open expressions of both sexual and platonic love—operate as micro-ceremonies, "as an expressive rejuvenation and reaffirmation of the moral values of the community."[2]

Perhaps the most obviously prevalent form of bodily communication at a Gathering is hugs. If you are open to them, you will receive many hugs from strangers. At my first several National Gatherings, there was a man who even called himself "Free Rainbow Hugs" and who walked around the Gathering yelling "Free Rainbow hugs!" and hugging anyone and everyone. At the 2012 Gathering, the influence of a younger generation's culture was evident in the phrase "Hug Life" (a play on "thug life") written with permanent marker on many people's stomachs; these people welcomed the hugs they received because of the written invitation. Short conversations may start and end with hugs, and group hugs are not an uncommon sight or activity. The simple touch of hugging, freely offered and freely given, helps to connect all sorts of different folks and heightens the sense of connectivity that each feels in turn.

In addition to hugs, eye contact is a simple nonverbal form of communication that is unusually common at a Rainbow Gathering. In contrast to Babylon, where people pass each other without acknowledgment as common practice, it is customary to acknowledge everyone you pass at a Gathering, looking them in the eye and perhaps offering a simple greeting. Direct eye contact and common acknowledgment, of course, also make people feel more connected. These basic exchanges between humans invoke emotional reactions of collectivity consistent with the form of social interchange.[3]

The culture of Rainbow is one of open contact and communication. People will often sit down with strangers for a rest along the trail, and if you sit down alone someone will likely soon join you. People feel welcome and willing to join a lone stranger to engage in positive, friendly interchanges that bolster the collective sentiment experienced at a Gathering.[4]

Nakedness, although technically illegal on public lands, is accepted at a Gathering, and this acceptance also contributes to the developed sense of collectivity. Some people wear very little, nothing but a loincloth, shorts, or an open robe. Many women walk around topless, but staring and gawking are not culturally appropriate (although direct compliments about someone's general beauty arguably are). The open acceptance of naked bodies is a part of the broader, pervasive culture of acceptance.

In addition to the clear examples of hugs, eye contact, and nakedness, there are many other forms of nonverbal communication and bodily interaction that contribute to the culture of Rainbow Gatherings and help to heighten the sense of collective connectedness experienced by many who gather. Some other specific forms of bodily communication that contribute to the energy of the Gathering involve participation, including perhaps unexpected or unusual forms of participation such as shouting, storytelling, trading, and doing drugs. These and other collective, bodily ways of communicating at a Rainbow Gathering contribute to a culture of sharing, where people are open to give to and receive from one another. The heightened sense of connectivity at a Rainbow Gathering is at least partially crafted by these cultural forms of bodily communication.

Participation

Participation is key at a Rainbow Gathering—a Gathering simply would not be possible without the hundreds of people who volunteer to carry supplies, collect firewood, cook meals, carry water, and help out in many other ways. Participation is even sometimes referred to as "the Rainbow way," and participation is an important part of the sense of collectivity and connection that develops among those who gather. According to Michael Niman, "Rainbows are volunteers, working without any regulatory mechanism to monitor their commitment. For Rainbows, like many successful communities . . . 'participation in the great communal enterprise . . . was its own reward and generated its own motivation.'"[5] In other words, "Everyone can do their own thing, but at the same time, everyone does everyone's thing."[6]

Sharing, an elder that I met at the 2012 National Gathering, called it "the miracle of volunteerism." Sharing is a stocky middle-aged woman who was wearing a long tie-dyed cotton dress, dangling feather earrings, and expensive hiking boots. We were talking beside her car in the parking lot near "not front gate again," where many of the elders at the Gathering were camped. She said that at a Rainbow Gathering, "You can do what you want, stop when you want, and feel good about whatever it is that you're doing for the Family. There's an openness here—an openness to contributing, to participation, to communication, that you don't find anywhere else."

There are many ways to directly participate at a Rainbow Gathering, many more ways than are presented to individuals in mainstream society. For many of the people I've talked to at Rainbow Gatherings who spend their days actively participating in the organization and systems of Rainbow, participation is indeed its own reward. People are energized by their own ability to meaningfully contribute, and voluntarism offers its own high. The energetic reward of participation, the sense of personal satisfaction and connection to the community that it provides, is itself the product of interaction.

At a Gathering, people are openly thanked and praised for participating. Participation becomes significant in contributing to the crafted sense of collectivity through social interaction; its meaning is "diffusely located in the flow of events in the encounter and becomes manifest only when these events are read and interpreted for the appraisals expressed in them."[7] A group sitting in a kitchen might shout "Loving you, brothers!" to a group of men hauling food or water. Someone might serenade you with an impromptu song about the Rainbow Way as you're picking up trash. Vocalized appreciation is a part of the culture of open communication.

In addition to contributing to the collective energy of a Gathering through the responses of thanks, praise, and positivity that it brings, participation offers other rewards at a Gathering. Helping with a kitchen often means having access to the best food at the kitchen, as only volunteers are allowed to scavenge the supply tent and some of the best treats are made exclusively for the kitchen crew's enjoyment. While Rainbow attempts to create a world of equal humans, there is certainly some differential access to resources, and some of this is based on participation. Kitchens often receive kick-downs of tobacco, extra good food, or even drugs, which are saved exclusively for kitchen crew, and these also help incentivize some participants.

Butterfly Bill is direct in describing his own strategic participation on kitchen crews during his first several Rainbow Gatherings:

> There was more of a chance that I would be there at the times food became ready, and I could come in behind the bliss rail and get served without having to stand in line, and I would get larger servings. I also got in on it if somebody prepared on a little fire off to the side a special treat, like bacon and eggs, or hamburger. And if a joint or pipe went around, it was passed to me without my having to ask. I would be "one of the crew" and have privileges not enjoyed by people who just walked in from the trail.[8]

Sometimes, these kick-downs and incentives are a part of the cultural expression, call it truth or myth, of the Gathering. At my very first National Gathering, someone told me,

> You know there are undercovers [referring to undercover law enforcement officers] out here. So if you ever want to offer to share a bowl [referring to a pipe packed with marijuana] with someone out here, which is always a really nice thing to do and greatly appreciated, here is the most important tip: smoke with the guys and gals who are hard at work. Undercovers aren't gonna be hauling food and water. They'll be the ones walking around in clean tennis shoes, not doing nothing. But all those folks that are helping, they're good Family. Now there's my tip to keep you safe.

At the 2012 Gathering, I heard a talkative woman who called herself Abbey Road tell a first-timer who had just arrived to the Gathering twenty minutes prior, "The mad doser is here! He's always here by now. So, what that means is, you gotta be nice to everyone. And always help. That's how you get dosed. And even if you don't get dosed, you'll feel good and you'll get high on that, you'll be giving off positive energy and will receive it back in turn. You know?" That same day, I heard a man say, "Down at O.P.M. kitchen tonight, the password is firewood! Collect as much firewood as you can and take it to the kitchen. Tell them the password, and you'll get dosed." Truth or myth, I bet they had more than enough firewood that night.

Participation is, for some, a means to healing. Rainbow Gatherings arguably offer a space for healing for those who need it; some people come "to heal from mental and spiritual wounds that they had suffered in Babylon, and to find new strength."[9] Junkies come to get off dope, alcoholics come to get away from drinking, people who are depressed or in need come to connect with others and have their spirits lifted. This is a part of what the culture of Rainbow provides. Participation is, for some, a very real means to healing. A man who calls himself Rascal once shared the following story:

> You know, I'm a healer, and one of the ways I participate here is by offering healing. Yesterday, I was talking with someone who has been going through some serious depression issues. That man confided that his mother had recently died. So the only thing I could do was tell the story of my own mother's death, and try to relate with him through his pain, and tell him about my own grieving process, which was a real rocky road, you know? So I told him all this stuff, really opened my heart and my own stories to him. And we connected through it, and he was touched. And it's this guy's first Gathering, and so I told him, "While you're here, every time you see someone needing help, or water or supplies that need to get carried down the trail, act like your mother told you to do it. And do it in honor of her." The next day, I saw that guy helping three other guys with a real heavy load, and he was smiling. You know? It's the healing of the mind and the spirit; they are the hardest to heal, but we can do that here.

In Rainbow culture, participation is both a way of connecting to one another and a means of personal healing. Physical participation is viewed as spiritual practice, a form of contribution but also of prayer, similar to the Buddhist principle and practice of Right Livelihood.[10] Further, the offering of healing space provides another means through which people connect and experience connection. The idea that people are capable of healing, that they can come to this space to heal and that the energy of the space itself can contribute to the healing process, is part of the culture of acceptance and tolerance.

There are many forms of participation that do not involve heavy loads or hard work that also contribute to the connectivity and positivity that many feel. Playing music is an honored form of participation. People play and sing for those gathered around bliss pits, for those digging shitters, and for those waiting in line for food. They play familiar tunes or spontaneous songs to express their ideas. I once heard a man singing the following tune while carrying a heavy load up a trail: "Everyone's in love with life, they just don't know it yet. Everyone is powerful, they might not know it yet."

Participating in conversations and activities with groups of strangers is also an important form of contribution. Games like Pocket Trash (fairly self-explanatory, where people stop you to take the trash that's accumulated in your pocket), Random Pocket Trade (where people trade two random items from their pockets), and Joke, Toke, or Smoke ("tolls" where people will ask you for one of the three in order to pass) contribute, as do other forms of collective expression like sweat lodges, yoga classes, and talent shows.

One evening at the 2012 Gathering, I was sitting in main meadow waiting for main circle to start. People were clustered sporadically throughout the meadow, chatting or playing music or sitting silently. Focalizers who were helping to organize the meal were standing and conversing in the middle. Seven of the folks standing in the middle of the meadow formed their own little circle, put their hands across one another's shoulders, and started an "affirmation circle." As they went around speaking and repeating one another's words, I heard things like

One alone: "I affirm."
The rest responding: "I affirm."
One alone: "That I am me, and you are you."
The rest repeating.
This pattern continued with: "Yet we are here."
"To see the ways."
"That I am you, and you are me!"
"I affirm."

Then it was the next person in the circle's turn, and that person said, followed by the rest repeating

"I affirm."

"That all things."

"Are made of the same stuff."

"Are made of one light."

"Human and animal."

"Living and non-living."

"Of the same energy."

"All deserve respect."

"I affirm."

And so on, around the circle.

When you start to look for them, you recognize that participatory forms of interaction that contribute to a heightened sense of connection and collectivity surround you at a Rainbow Gathering. In the participatory culture of Gatherings, there are so many things to do and ways to participate for everyone. This is what makes the participatory culture work, both practically and energetically. There's active physical work, but there's also a need for focalizers and facilitators. Some people enjoy the physical exercise of hauling food, water, and firewood; people who like to cook can always find a kitchen to help; other people prefer helping with organization or coordination. People with artistic propensities can make signs; people with healing and medical experience can volunteer with CALM; people with loud voices can find ways to be helpful making announcements to large circles or yelling "Six up!" or "Circle!" or "Free food in the woods!" Musicians can make music, and dancers can dance. Simply carrying a plastic bag on a walk and yelling "Pocket trash!" is an honorable way to participate. People who like to connect with one another through affirmation circles, sweat lodges, or council meetings can participate in these ways, while others participate by quietly doing dishes or digging shitters. There is something for everyone to do to contribute. This is related to both the material systems and the cultural system: the material systems themselves are low-tech and require much human involvement and input, and the cultural system emphasizes the ability and importance of people contributing in many diverse ways.

Further, there is immediate gratification in participation. You can see very quickly how you've made a difference when a kitchen crew gets excited about a food delivery. You hear it when other gatherers thank you as you are carrying a heavy load or immediately after sharing in a long, expressive group hug. In mainstream society, it takes much longer to be rewarded for work (at least two weeks for a paycheck) and the reward might not have much meaning in the context of what was done. Perhaps this is why some of the folks who come to Gatherings—the jobless, the homeless, or the otherwise "unproductive" in Babylon—are incredibly productive participants in the systems and culture of the Rainbow Gathering. People who cannot or do not actively or successfully participate in mainstream American society through jobs, paychecks, and mortgage payments are often the most involved in and most impacted by the Rainbow Gathering experience.

Participation at a Rainbow Gathering is entirely free; there are no rules for participation, and anyone can participate in anything at any time. This type of freedom, the freedom to directly and immediately impact your world in any way you choose, is incredibly empowering. At the 2012 National Gathering, a brother named A.C. talked about his inability to "get anything done" in Babylon, in contrast to a Gathering. He said, "For a long time I had a job working IT. . . . At Rainbow I'm with people on my level. Rainbow is the only place I feel like people love me. They'll say it, and I'll tell them back. It's good to exercise those neural pathways. I don't get that anywhere else." Cowboy, whose specialty at the 2012 Gathering was making coffee nonstop for all those who wanted it and always being willing to share in friendly exchanges around his fire pit while it brewed, said, "There's people like me that can't function in society. But I can serve coffee here." A full-time traveler who calls himself Steps to Freedom said, while frying a skillet full of potatoes over a fire, "I was always broke while I was in Babylon. I wasn't good at it. I'm good at this."[11]

As one observer of the 2012 National Gathering wrote, mainstream society cannot comprehend "what makes people like Christopher do what he does. A wanderer from Arizona, Christopher was busy Saturday, picking up other people's trash—without grumbling, without being told, without being paid. That is the answer worthy of pursuit, and worthy of emulating."[12] In our own society, productive participation usually involves a pretty narrow scope: we learn to go to work to make money to feed, clothe, and support ourselves and perhaps (if we're lucky) our families. We cannot freely and effectively participate in a community of people working together to meet one another's needs through common efforts and communal rewards. The desire for recognition (of our ability to meaningfully contribute, among other things) is a fundamental human wish,[13] and Rainbow Gatherings allow individuals to meaningfully participate, receive positive recognition for their many diverse forms of contribution, and "achieve an equilibrium which their society [i.e., Babylon], except under extraordinary circumstances, does not provide for them."[14]

There are a seemingly endless number of ways to contribute to the material and cultural ritual of a Rainbow Gathering. Some forms of participation may seem more surprising than others. A few potentially unexpected ways that people participate in Rainbow Gathering culture and contribute to the heightened sense collective effervescence in this social world include collective shouting, storytelling, trade or bartering, and the consumption of drugs.

Yelling! Collective and Anonymous

Shouting and yelling together is one of the ways people participate in the unique culture of a Rainbow Gathering, connecting and creating a sense of collectivity beyond personal communication. This yelling is often collective, like the shouts of "We love you!" that, once started by one group, echo through the woods as people clustered in various kitchens and camps respond. When this happens, you have no idea who in particular is responding. The chants are anonymous, yet they are collective, and they contribute to the sense of collective connection.

Unlike the chants of "We love you!" that often echo through the woods, some of the yelling is about communicating something specific. Kitchens yell when food is available. People yell when it's time for main circle; the first people who gather at main circle belt out organized shouts of "Circle!" on some loud individual's count of three so that others throughout the woods know it's time for dinner. Nic at Night, the group of individuals who freely hand out tobacco, are notorious yellers, loudly shouting at all times of day and night, things like "Nic at night! Satellite! You need a cigarette, we got a cigarette, you got a cigarette, we need a cigarette!" Much of this yelling takes place at night, heightening the mystery and anonymity of it. People wander the trails looking for a midnight snack after hearing calls for free food in the woods permeating the darkness. The loud shouts of folks from Nic at Night remind all gatherers, even those that don't smoke, where they are and what is freely provided to them in this unique social world. Shouts of "We love you!" create an intensified sense of collective sentiment—people you don't even know, couldn't even identify by the light of day, and cannot see shouting, love you! In all cases (even when people respond in a mocking manner, such as yelling "We huff glue!"), these collective and anonymous shouts contribute to the collective energy that saturates the Gathering.

Fakelore: Storytelling and Sociability

One of the most unusual aspects of Rainbow culture is the myth-making and storytelling, the sharing of and belief in the fantastical and the magical. It's not just the "Rainbow rumors"—ideas or stories that spread and distort like a game of telephone being played among thousands of people in motion. It's not only the types of ideas common to counterculture or fringe society—the significance of the year 2012, that "9/11 was an inside job," or the evidence of extraterrestrial life—that are common here. I've heard people talk very seriously about sasquatches and Bigfoot, fairies and ghosts. I've heard fantastical stories about people's lives and their friends' lives. I've heard opinions regarding surprisingly different combinations of prophets or deities. I've heard multiple different versions of the same Rainbow tales, sometimes from the same person.

The Rainbow Family of the Living Light is itself deeply connected to a tale, called myth or "Fakelore"[15] by skeptics. In 1972, *Rolling Stone* reported,

> There are those who will tell you Barry E. Adams is a spiritual hustler, the Elmer Gantry of hip. Others know him as Barry Plunker, or just Plunker, and consider him a prophet. In 1969, Plunker had a prophetic vision. A great gathering of tribes, the 144,000 of God's elect mentioned in the Book of Revelations. The elect would all mass on Independence Day at the center of the universe—a spot which Arapaho legends conveniently fix at Table Mountain. The more Plunker talked about it to his tribe, the Rainbow Family of Living Light, the more real, the more inevitable the vision became. There are the Indian legends claiming the spirit of slain warriors will return to reclaim the Earth. The gathering of the tribes could be the peace dance the Hopi elders always talked about.[16]

This prophecy about the coming together of the Rainbow tribe to care for the Earth and practice peace does correspond to some general beliefs among those who attend Rainbow Gatherings. However, it is arguably more important as a symbol of the types of magical, mythical, and mystical stories that color conversation at a Gathering. These stories and tales are just another way to actively participate in Rainbow culture, another way the culture embraces openness and freedom. People share these stories within a social world where even the most fantastical ideas are given space for expression, and the expression in turn enhances the culture of freedom.

Yet I once heard someone in the parking lot of a Gathering say, "I'll bullshit, but I ain't gonna lie to you." The openness of expression is like the sociability of a cocktail party,[17] although the emotive level of connection is arguably much more intense for most people at a Gathering. People share for the sake of sharing, and sharing in mythical tales of fantastic and outrageous proportion is part of both common and purposeful practice at a Gathering, as it connects people more closely and more positively with one another.

Trade

Although Rainbow Gatherings are distinctively noncommercial, the practice of trading or bartering has always taken place. A physical space for trading arises organically at every Gathering, and people set out blankets covered with their "tradeables"—zu zus and lighters, knives and clothing, handmade crafts, rocks and gems, pipes and drugs, and all sorts of other things. For some people, this is their primary or favorite activity at the Gathering. Trade is a definite form of interaction at every Gathering.

The character of trade circles has changed over the forty-year history of Gatherings. First, they have changed spatially. Trade circles used to be actual circles, set off of the main trail somewhere in the woods. The trade circle at the 2002 National Gathering was like this; under the shade of the large trees, a short trail led to people gathered in a loose circle shape. Now, trade circles often involve a long row of blankets set out right on the main trail. At the 2012 Gathering, trade took place along the main trail right in the center of the Gathering, often causing a blocked path, claustrophobia, and frequent yells of "Make a hole!" as people attempted to disperse the congregated masses so that other people could continue walking down the trail.

Trade circles have also changed culturally. As an elder who calls himself Preacher told me, "You used to be able to bring nothing but a rock. Now they're like carnies. So aggressive, so particular, think everything they have is worth its weight in gold. And now there is a real currency, and it's green [this is a reference to marijuana]." Even some little children get zealously involved in the trade game, circling over the blankets like little capitalists always looking to profit (although not monetarily) off each trade.

Trade is a contested issue at Gatherings. Some gatherers think that the profiteering aspect of trade that focuses on exploitation and advantage is contrary to the noncommercial spirit of the Gathering, while others complain that traders don't help with the basic needs of the Gathering like cooking food, hauling water, or chopping firewood. Butterfly Bill describes it this way: "Trading Circle was like the red light district in a Babylon town to some gatherers, a place where good and spiritual people didn't go, and a blight upon the community whose removal would leave the gathering a better place. But like A-Camp it couldn't be eradicated in the anarchy."[18]

Trade is an especially contested issue at the beginning and the end of a Gathering. Trading too early is perceived as laziness because there's so much work to be done in establishing the systems necessary to support the main event. Trading after July 7 is contested for much the same reason. At the 2012 National Gathering, people who were still setting out blankets to trade on July 8 were greeted with hostile shouts of "Go home!" from some clean-up crew participants.

For some people, trade is the most enjoyable part of the Gathering and their primary Gathering activity. For others, it is too dangerously close to the exploitative systems of acquisition that dominate mainstream society. Some people think traders are lazy (too lazy to participate in other ways); other people compare them to businesspeople or vultures. Yet despite the controversies surrounding it, trade is a significant form of interaction in Gathering culture. The presence of a trade circle, and the evolving character and centrality of it, influences the ways people interact for both those who participate and those who do not.

Drugs

Illegal drugs, particularly marijuana, hallucinogens, and others (but not generally opiates or methamphetamine) are fairly commonplace at a Gathering. These events are not primarily about the consumption of drugs; there are many people at Gatherings who do not partake and drugs are arguably not of central importance to Rainbow culture. However, mind-altering substances are relatively common and treated relatively casually at a Gathering, and they can certainly have an effect on the sense of collective effervescence experienced by participants.[19]

Victor Turner, an anthropologist who spent his career studying the emotional and social aspects of ritual and who used the word *communitas* to capture something similar to Emile Durkheim's concept of collective effervescence, "explicitly linked the experience of communitas with such things as ingestion of psychotropic drugs and rhythmic stimulation through singing and dancing."[20] Drugs, drumming, and dancing are indeed common forms of participation at a Gathering. Here, the key point is not the personal effects or relative merits of taking drugs but how they are taken: communally.

Marijuana is the most common illegal substance at a Gathering, and consumption is well suited to the communal culture. One joint or pipe is passed in a circle, rather than everyone having their own as with cigarettes or drinks. People stop to smoke together along the sides of trails at procrastination stations or "roadblocks." If you see people smoking, it is perfectly acceptable to stop and join them. You are not likely to be turned away, even by complete strangers, as it is part of the sharing and connected culture of a Gathering to be obliged to oblige when it comes to smoking marijuana (especially if you are an active participant, helpful, or perceived as attractive). People will "fish" for pot, tying an empty pipe to a string attached to a stick like a fishing pole. Other people will occasionally "fish" for people to smoke with, tying a full pipe in a similar way and waiting for someone to notice. People openly share marijuana, and the experience of smoking is a collective, communal one.

Other drugs are also shared in a somewhat communal fashion. Since money is not an accepted form of currency at a Gathering, people don't openly buy drugs. Drugs are traded for or even given freely. Stories of "mad dosers" giving away drugs (particularly LSD) to many different people are common. Thus, people are often high on the same drug at the same time, given to them by someone they may have never met. It is the sharing of drugs, rather than the simple consumption of them, that makes them an integral part of Rainbow Gathering culture.

A Culture of Sharing: My Rainbow Birthday

I celebrated my birthday at the 2012 National Rainbow Gathering, and the story of my day helps to demonstrate the culture of open participation, bodily connection, and sharing that exists at a Gathering. Before arriving at the Gathering, I had decided that I wanted to give away cake on my birthday. Many people come to the Gathering with something they want to share with other people; I've been given stickers, glow sticks, candy, fruit, and many other little gifts from people who come with enough of something to pass out to strangers along the trail. I decided that I wanted to share birthday cake.

I spent the night before my birthday baking cakes in my RV, frosting them and cutting them into tiny little pieces the next day. As Dave and I walked down the trail, I approached the strangers who were already making eye contact, smiling, and greeting me (because of the culture of this unique event, but probably also because I was carrying cake). I got so much joy out of watching their eyes and smiles widen as they noticed the cake and heard me say, "It's my birthday. Would you like a piece of cake?" Very few people refused the offer (some gatherers avidly avoid sugars or non-plant-based food products), and most responded with hugs and cheers of "Happy birthday!" Some offered me little gifts like pretty rocks, mini candy bars, and blackberries picked fresh from the bushes in the meadow in return for the sweet treat.

Handing out free cake to strangers would be a truly unusual way to celebrate a birthday in Babylon, but at a Rainbow Gathering it fits neatly into the culture of connection and sharing. No one asked why on earth I would do such a thing, and no one treated me with skepticism or fear. Instead, the culture of openness, connectivity, and appreciation allowed us all (both the givers and the receivers) to enjoy the processes and interactions of sharing.

By the time we made it back to our tent, we were out of cake. But we had gotten to know the folks at Montana Mud during our short time at the Gathering, and since they knew it was my birthday, they prepared their own celebration. As we walked up to the kitchen that evening, I heard Lazy shout, "Hey Mudders! I told you we had a birthday in the house today; well here she is!" Several familiar faces from the kitchen and many others I had never seen yelled "Happy birthday!" or came over to greet me with a hug. A woman I had never met gave me a birthday gift, a small piece of beautiful fabric. And there was more cake—the kitchen had made several rich chocolate cakes to share with late-night visitors to the kitchen in honor of my birthday. Dave and I were given two enormous pieces, and there was plenty for everyone there. We spent the evening sitting around the kitchen bliss pit eating the delicious cake, engaging in casual conversation with friends and strangers, listening to two men sing and play guitar, and enjoying a visit from the mail carrier looking to deliver some letters.

Well after dark, to my complete surprise, the happy birthday song was sung. There were still about forty people sitting around the bliss pit and others in nearby camps, gathered together at the tepee on top of the hill, or congregated in and around individual tents. When Lazy and Jackson started singing, everyone chimed in. The song was coming from unknown voices off in the distant darkness as well as those seated right around me. Most of the people singing didn't even know my name, so there was a pause and a quieting when they got to that part of the song, followed by several people shouting my name after they'd heard it sung by those who knew.

It was quite an experience, sharing in that moment of communal participation and caring connection with so many complete strangers. To me, it helps reveal the very heart of the Rainbow experience. At a Rainbow Gathering, people connect through sharing freely, communicating openly, and both giving and receiving. To participate in the sharing is to contribute to and to feel the collective connectivity.

The Big Event: July 4, 2012 (and After)

The height of connectivity at a Rainbow Gathering occurs on July 4. For the few days and nights prior to it, the Gathering reaches its pinnacle of population and energy. Some people stay up all night drumming and dancing, shouting and singing, and visiting kitchens serving zu zus. A local reporter described the night of July 3 at the 2012 National Gathering this way:

> They were drumming in honor of the full moon. Hundreds of people gathered tightly around a huge fire pit, watching the embers fly into the sky. Some danced around the edges, gyrating to the beat in various states of nudity. Others sprawled out in the grass, intermittently bursting into cheers for two women who danced nearby with hoops of fire. In other places scattered through the forest, smaller groups of musicians and participants created the same shared energy.[21]

Then, on the morning of the Fourth, the woods are (almost) silent. Not everyone participates in the morning of silence, because Gatherings don't mean the same thing to everyone who gathers and because no one is going to police or enforce the silence (other than the occasional "shhh!"). The function of the silence, according to the Rainbow Family, is to "pray for peace"—it is a morning spent in silent prayer. Yet sociologist Robert Merton emphasized that the most important contribution of sociology is the study of latent or unintended consequences,[22] and an underlying function of the silence is to demonstrate the unspoken connectivity between those who gather. The ritual of silence "serves some intrinsic, instrumental purpose. The ritual is used to focus attention, to help create a situation that allows total absorption."[23] People continue to make eye contact and smile at one another, or they may bow to say (without saying) "Namaste." The crafted collectivity reaches its peak, heightened by the thousands of people who communicate in silence.

On the morning of the Fourth, Dave and I started walking the trails early to observe the ritual. We passed numerous people, silently communicating, as they ate breakfast at kitchens and made their way toward the main meadow. We found a comfortable rock just off the main trail to sit and watch as hundreds of people passed by us on their way to the main circle. On this day of celebration, people "put on their psychedelic Sunday best."[24] Costumes of colorful clothing; long, flowing skirts on both men and women; face paint; and butterfly wings are fairly common anytime at a Gathering, but they are most common on the Fourth. People are dressed in their most colorful, celebrative rainbow clothing, tutus and muumuus and tie-dye of all sorts. One man in a monk-like smock carried a handmade, cardboard sign that said "I love you family" as he silently walked the trails, seemingly involved in his own form of meditation that also touched all those he passed.

At Rainbow Noon, the hundreds or thousands of people who gather in the main meadow form a circle, stand, and join hands for a collective Om. The Om circle usually corresponds with a parade of children from Kid Village coming into the center of the circle. A woman at the 2012 National Gathering described Gatherings as a prayer for peace that begins with the creation of this unique social world, this community, and its rituals and climaxes with the events of the Fourth. She said, "The beginning of the prayer is pretty much with creating the community together. . . . The circle [on July 4] is the culmination of creating that community, all of which is a prayer for peace."[25]

At some Gatherings I've attended, the main circle stretches as one single circle of connected people across vast meadows, sometimes over terrain that makes it impossible to even see the entire unbroken chain. Other times, the main meadow is too small for one large circle, and circles form within circles. At the 2012 Gathering, the main meadow was even too small for this, so the connected hands were joined in one large spiral. People stood close to one another, spiraling in, and the energy was incredibly strong. The children's parade danced all the way through and around the spiral, and the Om seemed to last a very long time.

As the resonating sounds of the Om begin to fade, people raise their joined hands and together yell, shout, and holler for joy. Then, a large drum circle begins in the middle of the meadow. In the hot air of the Tennessee summer, many people stripped down and danced naked around the drummers. There is an incredible air of celebration that lasts throughout the day and into the night as people dance, make music, and celebrate in the woods.

The day after (July 5), the energy of the Gathering has shifted. It feels as if some of the energy is drained or at least transformed. People are quieter. They continue to make eye contact but may be less inclined to speak. The people who do say "Hello, sister" or "Loving you, brother" say it more quietly, with an air that feels simultaneously less energized and more intimate. It is impossible to sustain the energetic high of collective effervescence for long.[26]

The material organization and interaction rituals of the Gathering begin to shift after July 4. Many people go home, likely changed by the experience, at least for a while. People tell me that they return home wanting to say "Hello" and "Lovin' you" to their friends and colleagues, or with the impulse to pick up the small pieces of trash that used to go unnoticed on sidewalks or in parks. I too have experienced these things. While many begin their journeys back to wherever they came from, others remain in the woods, preparing to dismantle this ephemeral social world, perhaps only to travel on to the next National Forest where they establish and experience it again.

Connecting through Conflict

Of course, not everyone actively participates in the collective ritual of a Rainbow Gathering. Some people aren't silent on July 4 and some people mock the shouts of "We love you!" that echo through the woods. Some people don't help and thus don't feel the heightened energy and connectivity that come from helping. Yet the forms of communication and connection that create such effervescence at a Rainbow Gathering work to craft a sense of collectivity, even though not everyone who gathers participates.

One reason for this is that the forms of expression and communication are intentionally peaceful, respectful, and loving. There is intention in the ritualized aspects of Rainbow culture.[27] People say "Hello family" to the Forest Service rangers who walk through the Gathering, even though the rangers technically have the authority to remove gatherers at any time. People teach the locals, who may not know about or understand Rainbow culture, the ways of interacting in this unique world. Shanti Sena, the voluntary peacekeepers who use loving language and nonviolence to diffuse negative interactions, provide an alternative to physical or legal enforcement. Interaction at a Gathering is intended to be peaceful and respectful, and this is the approach taken to interaction even in nonreciprocal situations.

Another reason that those who don't participate in the connectivity of a Gathering aren't sanctioned, imposed upon, or considered a threat for Gathering culture is that freedom is the ultimate value of this culture. This freedom is limited in practice only when individual actions impinge on the freedom of others or negatively impact the natural environment; individual freedom of expression in clothing choices, communication styles, action, and interaction is key to the experience of community in this unique social world. People are free to refrain from participating in the silence of July 4 and are free to yell "We huff glue!" in response to calls of "We love you!" People are free to stay silent during Om circles or to not attend main circle meals at all. People are free to refrain from participating in affirmation circles, the freely exchanged hugs, and any other Rainbow activity. People are free to connect to whatever extent and in whatever ways they choose. This value of freedom creates a precarious balance in this social world, but it also contributes to the experience of connectivity. A Rainbow Family elder, an older man using a walking stick and wearing a black leather vest, black top hat, and several long beaded necklaces, once told me, "We are all sovereign autonomous beings. But we are also all connected beings, connected to the one life force, the one energy that is the universe. Any attempt to find God that ignores the inevitable duality in every human being will fail. We only become truly sovereign entities by recognizing our connectedness."

Bodily Rituals of Connection

A Rainbow Gathering is a unique, temporary social world in which people communicate, act, and interact in ways that are different than in everyday, mainstream society. The National Rainbow Gathering offers a yearly ritual in which thousands of diverse people come together to participate in a collective experience. A friend of mine, a woman in her forties who attended her first Rainbow Gathering a decade ago, told me, "I showed up all closed and cold, not even really realizing it. By the end of the Gathering, I was wandering around bright-eyed saying 'Lovin' you' to everyone I passed, just like the people I'd gawked at my first day there." A woman in her twenties who came to the 2012 Gathering from Brooklyn, New York, told me, "It's just so refreshing to be in a place where people are open, and kind, and loving. It's like the exact opposite of where I've been living, and it's amazing how I felt myself shutting down there while I've opened up so quickly here."

The nonverbal forms of communication, the ways people connect with one another through common action and practice, contribute to the collective effervescence that many experience during this ritual event. They act, to borrow a term from sociologist Erving Goffman, as forms of *social ritualization*, standards of bodily and verbal behavior that serve a particular function in the interaction order and help give meaning to interactive communication.[28] The social encounters[29] that take place at a Rainbow Gathering contribute to the positive energy and sense of connectivity experienced by participants. The forms of interaction contribute to the emotional experience. Hugs and other ways of connecting through bodily communication such as making or serving a meal, hauling water for a kitchen, stopping to talk with a friendly looking group, or sharing a joint with strangers are mini-rituals that contribute to the larger ritual of a Gathering and the heightened sense of collective effervescence that people experience.

Further, those who don't buy into the collective forms of experience and connection—from the Forest Service rangers who are there to work to the drunks who are gruff and violent rather than peaceful and loving to the young folks who come just to party—also contribute to the collective experience through their very freedom of choice not to participate in particular aspects of Rainbow culture. Rainbow Gatherings are many things indeed. They are about practicing an environmentally responsible leave-no-trace camping ethic. They are about getting high on marijuana and mushrooms while in communion with nature, but not getting drunk (although, for some, Gatherings are about getting drunk). They are about spirituality and prayer. They are about healing the hearts of humans who seek it. They are rhythmic celebrations of drumming and dancing. They are practices in communal, nonhierarchical living in which basic needs are freely met. Yet, above all, they are rituals of freedom. Participation in the collectivity happens freely, and even the people and incidents that challenge the crafted collective sentiment contribute to the effervescence, the sense of connectivity felt by those who dwell in the ritual experience.

CHAPTER 7

THE CHURCH OF NATURE

RAINBOW CONNECTIONS WITH THE EARTH

For those that experience Rainbow Gatherings as a spiritual event, the natural environment is an important object of spiritual significance; for many gatherers, the natural world is sacred. Rainbow land is itself in a natural setting without transmission lines, telephone poles, asphalted roads, or permanent buildings of any kind. Rainbow land is referred to as a church by many gatherers, who use phrases like "Keep guns out of the church!" and "No alcohol in the church." At the 2012 National Gathering, I saw several bumper stickers on cars in the parking lot that read, "Nature is my church." Also at that Gathering, I saw the satirical "'test'" posted on a sign by the information booth that identified both "exploration of our National Forests" and "Religious group that travels to the cathedral of nature to pray for world peace July 4th" (as well as "Preparation for living in the wild so we'll be ready when society collapses") as accurate (although not comprehensive) descriptions of the Rainbow Family and their Gatherings. Many of the people who gather share the belief that nature serves as a sacred site for these spiritual events and that the natural world more broadly is a sacred place to be treated with love, care, and respect.

This element of Rainbow Gathering culture, the relationship to nature as sacred, is loosely connected to Native American traditions[1] as well as the philosophies of ecocentrism[2] and deep ecology.[3] Certainly not everyone who attends a Rainbow Gathering holds these beliefs, but for many of the people who come to Gatherings, humans are but one among many species deserving of equal treatment. Furthermore, many gatherers believe that nature's elements, processes, and rhythms are the most valuable expressions of Earth's potential and the best teachers to guide human action and interaction. This suggests that human action must be geared toward caring for and respecting the Earth rather than exploiting and degrading it. A common Rainbow chant, lyrics of unknown origin, often vocalized to the beat of a drum circle at a Gathering, demonstrates this orientation:

The Earth is our Mother
We must take care of her
The Earth is our Mother
We must take care of her

The Sky is our Father
We must take care of him
The Sky is our Father
We must take care of him

The sacred ground we walk upon
With every step we take
The sacred ground we walk upon
With every step we take

People at a Gathering value nature's resources as sacred gifts. This is demonstrated by many common Rainbow practices: all food served at the dinner circle is vegan or vegetarian, natural and herbal remedies are offered as common practice at CALM and are often offered with prejudicial preference over standard over-the-counter medical remedies. People are much more likely to eat a clove of garlic than to spray OFF to deter mosquitoes (such highly chemically laden products are often looked down upon). The Rainbow Family has a document called the "mini-manual" available at the information booth at every National Gathering. While not an official document of any kind, this little booklet serves as a sort of orientation packet for first-time attendees. In the mini-manual, a section on "respecting the land" comes second only to the first section called "finding your way home," before even a description of governance and decision making. This section reminds gatherers that

We gather in the **Cathedral of Nature** & *disturb the environment as little as possible.* . . . If you pack it in, you must pack it out. If you don't, someone else will have to do it for you. Hence, pick up trash left by others who have not yet learned the Rainbow Way. Educate them with kindness. It's good for the soul. *The earth is our mother, we must take care of her!!*[4]

In some versions of the mini-manual you will also find the following pledges: "*We pledge* to walk lightly on the earth. *We pledge* to respect and care for each other and for all living things."

This worldview suggesting that nature is a sacred place deserving of respect and care and that nature (not corporations) is the best provider of human needs shapes how the material systems that support dwelling at a Gathering are constructed and organized as well as reinforces and even heightens the cultural experiences of the event. Because nature is sacred, and Rainbow Gatherings take place in a natural setting, the event itself is sacred too. People participate in this ritual event in part because of their orientation to the Earth upon which it occurs.

Earth-Wise Responsibility and the Freedom to Dwell

Many (but certainly not all) of the people who attend Rainbow Gatherings are or strive to be what I call earth-wise—because they see the natural world as sacred, they aim to understand the environment in order to limit the harm they cause while dwelling on this hallowed ground. This relationship to the natural world is not limited to the National Forest site of the Gathering; all of nature is considered sacred, deserving of care and respect. This cultural relationship to nature reveals itself through both levels of knowledge and awareness about the environment among gatherers and the actions they take to behave with an earth-wise responsibility.

At a Rainbow Gathering, you might have the opportunity to participate in workshops on natural medicine and herbal remedies, alternative forms of food production from permaculture growing techniques to small-scale canning and fermentation, or local botany. The vast majority of attendees would almost certainly agree that climate change is a serious threat; that fossil fuels are a bad energy choice for a host of environmental, political, and even spiritual reasons; that renewable energy sources are a better alternative; and that the levels of material consumption dominating mainstream America are environmentally (as well as spiritually) harmful. Yet awareness of and connection to the environment permeate to a deeper, interpersonal level.

People at Rainbow Gatherings don't often talk about their lives in Babylon. While asking someone about their occupation or income may not necessarily be taboo, it is definitely not the typical way to start a conversation at Rainbow (as we do in Babylon, where the first question almost every stranger asks another is, "So, what do you do?"—meaning how do you earn a living, not what do you most enjoy in your life). Yet people are very likely to exchange knowledge of, information about, or tales about experiences in the natural world. People talk about the various water sources available at the Gathering and their relative cleanliness. They converse about the species of birds or trees that surround them. They share stories from times spent in other forests and landscapes they've seen. People are conscientious of the natural world around them, sharing what they've observed and learned and together watching the skies to talk about the weather. These conversations don't have the superficial trivialization you might imagine in a question like "What's the weather like where you're from? or "Think it's going to rain today?" Instead, people truly connect, sometimes on a deep level, by sharing what they've seen and learned in the natural world around them. Gatherers talk about the brightness of the stars, the cycles of the moon, the habits and benefits as well as the potential dangers of the plants and animals around them—connecting with one another via a connection to the natural world.

Both significant knowledge and responsible action are structurally conditioned necessities at a Rainbow Gathering. Without knowledge about how to find a clean water source and how to keep from polluting it, gatherers could make one another very sick. Without knowledge about the plants that surround them, gatherers wouldn't know which ones to avoid (did you know some trees let off a smoke that is toxic when you burn them?) and which ones could enrich their lives (like the sassafras tree, the roots of which make a wonderful, potentially mind-altering tea). Knowledge of the natural world helps Rainbow gatherers prepare for the conditions of the specific site, keep supplies dry in the rain, and address potential causes of harm to one another. Further, earth-wise responsible action is a legal necessity for anyone camping in the National Forest, which re-quires that campers clean up after themselves. Given the somewhat contentious relationship between the National Forest Service and the Rainbow Family,[5] gatherers can help ease the tension by taking care of themselves and the mess they create without government intervention.

Yet the relationship to the natural world expressed by the Rainbow Family is about more than structural necessities or bureaucratic niceties; it is deeply entrenched in the cultural values and practices of this social world. It is through Rainbow Gathering culture that knowledge and awareness of the natural world become practice. Many of the cultural norms that prevail at a Gathering, and certainly the vast majority of those that are strong or enforced norms, are intended to limit the damage to the natural world caused by the event or to address issues of sanitation that arise when living with systems and practices so directly connected to the natural world. The only real limitations on individual behavior that exist at a Rainbow Gathering are related to treating the natural world with care.

If you camp too close to a stream and could potentially harm the delicate ecosystem or water source, no one (except a Forest Service ranger) can make you move your tent, but you will likely have many other gatherers approach you in attempt to persuade you. If you are caught defecating somewhere other than a communal shitter, you would face not only the potential embarrassment of being caught in the act but also a very angry crowd who would lecture you about the harm you could be causing the water and your fellow gatherers and express disapproval about your general disrespect for both the Earth and the humans around you. You may also get this lecture if you leave your dog's mess on the trail. If you smoke tobacco and leave the butt of a filtered cigarette on the ground, you will most certainly receive a look or two of scorn at the very minimum. More disruptive environmental acts like using a chainsaw or a gasoline-powered generator, or intentionally causing harm to any living thing, will definitely provoke nasty responses from others.

This is one of the only limits on complete individual freedom at a Gathering: do not harm the Earth. The mini-manual includes suggestions, requests, and expressions of cultural practice such as no campsite or latrine should be located above or within 300 feet of springs; never use soap in a water source; cut no living tree; when you build a fire, always have a shovel and at least five gallons of water nearby; do not litter; and never leave waste unburied. A section on "technology" reads, "*We welcome non-polluting, low energy technology* such as solar, wind-power, etc. Excepting flashlights, lanterns, & stoves, fuel-powered and electrically generated devices are not welcome!"[6]

Thus, in this anarchistic social world where almost anything goes, where people can do and say almost anything they please, wear what they want (including nothing), and be whatever they choose to be, this freedom comes with a responsibility: to act in an earth-wise manner. This is part of the cultural system unique to this social world: freedom comes with the responsibility to behave in ways that do not harm the Earth. When people use the phrase "Welcome home" at a Gathering, they are not simply suggesting that people are all there to dwell together for a little while or simply acknowledging the open, embracing culture of a Gathering. I believe they are also indicating another, lesser-used definition of home—"a place where something flourishes"—and expressing the belief that human beings and social systems can flourish only without exploitation of the natural world or one another.

The environmental values embedded in the cultural system of the Rainbow Family shape action and interaction within the social world of a Rainbow Gathering. Not everyone who attends consciously adopts these principles or values them through their practices. One of the most amazing things about a Rainbow Gathering is that anyone can attend, no one is turned away, and the people who come represent the whole spectrum of human beings and countercultural freaks. Not all of them care about the Earth, but the overall culture of the Gathering fosters earth-wise responsible behavior among those who gather.

Leave-No-Trace Ethic and Practice in Dismantling a Temporary Metropolis

One of the clearest examples of the environmental ethic that pervades Rainbow Family culture is the clean-up effort that takes place after the Gathering. After thousands of people have come to camp and all of the systems to support and maintain the event have been established, some gatherers voluntarily stay behind to practice leave-no-trace camping for the thousands of people who came to this temporary metropolis in the woods. An attendee who calls himself Anonymous said that the Rainbow Family "advocates the outdoor ethic of Leave No Trace, which means keeping the woods as pristine as possible."[7] As one reporter put it, "Many of those attending profess beliefs in environmental activism, and the gathering includes a volunteer team that stays behind to restore the space to its pre-event state."[8] One of the slogans written on signs hung throughout the Gathering is "If you're strong enough to pack it in, be loving enough to pack it out."

An estimated 6,500 to 7,500 people attended the 2012 National Rainbow Gathering, which took place in the Cherokee National Forest in Tennessee. After the climax of July 4, flocks of attendees began to leave and the volunteer clean-up crew began to spontaneously organize, with clean-up crew council meetings and individuals working alone and together to begin cleaning up all evidence of the humans that gathered in the previously uninhabited woods. On July 5, I heard a woman sitting along the main trail singing this song while strumming her guitar: "Pack it in, pack it out. And if you don't wanna pack it out, give it to us. Because we're clean-up crew, and we stay behind to clean up the woods, so give us all your shit, so we do it real good." By July 6, the population had decreased to an estimated 4,700.[9]

After the Vision Council begins on July 7—where the decision about where to hold next year's Gathering is made by consensus, a meeting that often takes several consecutive days—the entire mood of the Gathering shifts. The energy changes from joy and celebration to task-oriented action, where "basically, if you're here, you help."[10] By July 15, there were only an estimated 300–400[11] people left on site, and when the remaining gatherers finally deemed the site restored at the end of the month, there were only a few dozen people left.[12]

The people who stay behind take responsibility for making sure that every indication that the event even took place is gone before they leave.[13] Kitchen sites are "disappeared" so that you'd never know they had been there at all. Fire pits, compost pits, and shitters are filled in. Every last piece of trash is picked up and hauled away, dozens and dozens of trash bags' worth. Areas that were severely trampled are reseeded. All evidence of this temporary metropolis is removed.

Some people stay and help with clean up for several days, while others stay for several weeks. Tigger "is among a few dozen group members who remained behind to clean up trash, remove camp facilities and otherwise 'rehab' and return forest areas back to their original appearance and condition." He stayed behind to help with the entire clean-up and says it is "a labor of pride and love by Rainbow members." He said, "It's about taking only what you need when you're in this environment. And, when you're done, it's about giving back more than you've taken from here."[14] An attendee who calls himself Crash described it this way: "Staying behind to clean up the mess others made fulfills a need to give back."[15]

The people who are most active in dismantling the temporary metropolis created in the National Forest for this unique event are often those who can stay longer because they don't have careers or homes or traditional obligations to return to in Babylon. Many are full-time travelers. Yet these gatherers don't necessarily participate in clean-up out of a sense of caring, kindness, or obligation felt toward other people; they do a lot of complaining about the "weekend warriors" who come to Gatherings but don't participate in cleaning up, who leave their trash behind or don't bury any shitters or compost pits even though they used them. For most people who stay behind to "disappear" the Rainbow Gathering site, it is not a sense of responsibility or caring for other people that motivates participation in clean-up. It is about earth-wise responsible freedom, about stewardship of a sacred place. It is also about the self-empowerment that comes from the freedom and ability to meaningfully participate. For people who don't have a means of satisfying both their sense of freedom and their sense of worth outside a Rainbow Gathering, the opportunity to participate freely and to meaningfully contribute can provide profound emotional satisfaction.

A leave-no-trace ethic motivates the organization and practices of the material world of a Rainbow Gathering. A lot of knowledge goes into successfully practicing leave-no-trace camping for thousands of people. The clean-up crew debates what materials are safe or unsafe to burn (lots of clothes are left behind, but synthetic fabrics are not burned), how to best fill latrines and other pits (with mounds on top, rather than flat with the surface, so that there doesn't end up being sunken ground there over time), and how to best dispose of trash without upsetting local residents (usually, the necessary fees are paid to dump whatever isn't hauled away by gatherers at the local landfill using funds collected by the Magic Hat). There is an environmental ethic motivating action and interaction at a Rainbow Gathering based on earth-wise knowledge and the responsible use of it to best care for the sacred natural world.

Nature as Sacred

Many (but not all) who identify with the Rainbow Family consider nature to be sacred. Based on Emile Durkheim's conception of religion, nature is a sacred object for the Rainbow Family. The physical space of a Rainbow Gathering, in a natural environment, is itself considered sacred. Yet for those who recognize nature as sacred, it is more than the physical space itself or the objectified conception of nature that holds value. Human actions matter because they enter into and affect natural dynamics, and nature's processes are considered sacred. The processes of nature are understood as a dynamic, interactive collection of energies and beings. Humans must respect this dynamic nature for her very dynamics. Nature is not just a sacred object; nature is mother, nature is Gaia,[16] and nature's rhythms represent more possibility and potential than anything created by the humans of Babylon.

The material and cultural systems of a Rainbow Gathering are shaped by an underlying ethic of earth-wise responsible freedom, a consensus-based, leave-no-trace anarchy in which people are free to behave in any way except those that harm the Earth or one another. The view that nature is sacred and that natural dynamics and processes are sacred shapes the form of freedom that prevails within the culture of this unique ritual experience. At a Gathering, people are free to openly participate in the creation of this unique social world that respects nature as sacred. For many Gathering participants, the freedom to meaningfully shape the material, social, and spiritual experience of a Rainbow Gathering through earth-wise responsible action and interaction is a key aspect of this social world.

CHAPTER 8
CONCLUSION

CRAFTING COLLECTIVITY

Butterfly Bill wrote that Rainbow Gatherings are "a wild and crazy ride I take each year to discover things I can find nowhere else . . . a chance to test dreams by making them reality."[1] A unique social world constructed through interaction, Rainbow Gatherings are a temporary, reoccurring ritual event that creates a sense of collective effervescence among those who participate. The material and cultural systems of a Rainbow Gathering work together to contribute to the crafted sense of connected collectivity that many gatherers experience.

The constructed material and cultural systems of a Gathering, as well as the ways of acting and interacting that they facilitate and encourage, stand in radical contrast to those of mainstream society. Systems of meaning at a Gathering are markedly different from those in mainstream society. What can this unusual and countercultural world teach us about how societies work, materially and culturally, to come together into coherence?

This study demonstrates the important fact that collective effervescence is crafted through interaction. Other sociologists have studied interaction and its ritual elements.[2] The social worlds approach inspired by the Chicago school brings interaction to the center of the study of ritual, suggesting that the study of experiences of collective effervescence ought to focus on rituals of interchange, processes of spatial and material organization, and other forms of interaction that influence the crafting of collective effervescence.

Material and Cultural Systems as Ritual

The main argument throughout this work is that the organization of material systems shapes, in important ways often unbeknown to those who use them, the cultural systems in which we live, the cultural values we prioritize, and the ways we act and interact as both individual and social beings. Rainbow Gatherings are a unique social world in which the material systems that support these temporary forms of dwelling are deeply shaped by and actively work to reinforce the cultural system in which they are created. Simply put, the material systems of a Rainbow Gathering are freely available and freely provided through the voluntary efforts of those who gather. The cultural system of a Gathering is also free, open, and participatory.

Rainbow Gatherings are a social world involving unique ritual processes. Some sociologists and anthropologists have spent their lives studying unusual ritual events, and they suggest that all things social involve elements of ritual; social acts are ritual processes.[3] Going to church, brushing your teeth, flipping a light switch, and shopping for groceries are among many, many other social acts that all involve elements of ritual. In this study, we see that these rituals are reinforced by the material systems that support them and the ways these systems are organized.[4] Social life is inscribed and made meaningful through the daily actions enacted through ritual interaction with particular material systems.[5]

The technological structures that support human dwelling are shaped by and come to shape how we act and interact with one another. The physical systems at a Gathering, which are free and open and require interactive participation, support and even work to promote a cultural system that is also free and open and involves active engagement. The material structures that support life at a Gathering—the temporary water systems, free food provision and distribution, the construction and maintenance of sanitary facilities, freely provided health care and medical supplies, organization of the physical environment—are the tangible, physical things that make Gatherings happen. These material systems reinforce an intangible cultural system.

These technological structures require active participation, and they actively empower participants to engage with collective life in ways that enhance social connectivity. Both the material systems and the cultural systems contribute to the experience of collective effervescence, the feeling of social connectivity, shared by many gatherers. The material systems reinforce the cultural systems and contribute to the collective effervescence felt at this yearly ritual.

One could say that these material systems arose out of necessity, because Gatherings take place in the near wilderness, on National Forest land. Yet the fact that the Gathering takes place on public land is simply another structural reinforcement of the cultural values—free, noncommercial, open to all participants, and requiring the active involvement of participants themselves. There are an infinite number of ways to meet the needs of thousands of people gathering together, as demonstrated by other annual events like Burning Man and music festivals like Bonnaroo. People could pay for access and sustenance,[6] or kitchens could use a wide variety of more exclusive definitions of membership to limit who helps and who's fed. Rainbow Gatherings effectively demonstrate the link between material and cultural systems: how we choose to organize our technological systems affects how we act and interact with the systems that provide for our needs and comforts as well as how we act and interact with the natural world and one another.

This is not intended to be a deterministic argument that material systems cause social systems.[7] Yet they are certainly related; they reinforce and perpetuate one another. Mary Douglas, an anthropologist inspired by Durkheim's work, once wrote that understanding the relationship between the material and cultural world "demands an ecological approach in which the structure of ideas and of society, the mode of gaining a livelihood and the domestic architecture are interpreted as a single interacting whole in which no one element can be said to determine the others."[8] Studying Rainbow Gatherings illuminates the complex codetermining relationship between material systems and cultural systems. All material systems reinforce some particular cultural system and have a social outcome. At Rainbow Gatherings, both are open to all, require active participation, and emphasize care for the natural world. Both contribute to the ritual experience, shaping how individual people act and interact in this social world. At Rainbow Gatherings, material systems promote equality and equity, respect for the natural world and one another, and active, empowering engagement. Active participation in the material systems that support dwelling life reinforces a cultural system that empowers individuals to engage with the social world, which heightens their sense of connection and collectivity.

Here, you might ask, why does this matter? It matters because physical and material systems operate the same way in mainstream society. When we recognize that material systems reinforce cultural systems, we can begin to ask ourselves what kind of cultural systems we'd like to promote and what material systems are best attuned to them.[9] What are we emphasizing (what sort of cultural and social systems are we perpetuating) through the material systems of mainstream society? What sort of culture are they contributing to?

Consider the contrast between the material systems that support life at a Gathering and typical American dwelling. Can you have a conversation with the person who tapped the source of your drinking water to ask about cleanliness or filtration? Can you physically see how far away your waste is from your food or water supply or actively do anything to influence such decisions? Can you thank a restaurant for a delicious meal you didn't pay for by volunteering to wash some dishes? At a Rainbow Gathering, you can. Are you always fed when you're hungry, provided water when you're thirsty, or afforded care when you're sick, regardless of your ability to pay? At a Rainbow Gathering, you are. In Babylon, only the most economically fortunate are so privileged. Further, even the most economically advantaged are dependent upon technical experts, managers, and policy makers to determine whether their food, water, and systems of sanitation are safe.[10] The extent to which individual human beings get to influence, act upon, and participate in both the material and cultural systems at a Rainbow Gathering is simply unheard of in mainstream society. The material systems are low-tech and require a lot of human effort. The cultural system is one in which this effort is valued, appreciated, and even rewarded (but, importantly, not monetarily).

At a Rainbow Gathering, people use earth-wise means of collectively meeting the needs of sustenance in ways that reinforce a participatory and communal experience. Similarly, if you live on a commune, your food and housing and basic necessities are provided for collectively; this reinforces the collective experience. In contrast, if you live in mainstream America, you pay an economic, monetary price for all the basic necessities of food, light, warmth—all the means of comfort and well-being. This reinforces the solitary and individualistic capitalist experience.

Further, the material systems of mainstream American society all involve an imaginary "awayness" that simply does not exist.[11] When we flush our toilets, our waste becomes someone else's problem. When we brush our teeth, the wastewater we created simply "disappears." When we flip a light switch, we may never think about where the electricity is coming from or what it really takes to create it. When we shop for groceries, we very rarely know who grew, raised, slaughtered, processed, or produced the food we buy. Our material technologies, and our human and social relationships to them, require and reinforce our participation in rituals of alienation; it is alienation both from the natural environment and from one another.[12] Our material systems contribute to and reinforce this cultural relationship.

According to anthropologist Victor Turner, this is far from ideal. Instead, we should seek to have social structures—both material structures like the technological systems we use to provide light, warmth, food, and water and structural relationships like class—that serve in the creation of *communitas*, the experience of fundamental human connection.[13] Rainbow Gatherings arguably do just that, by establishing material systems that reinforce equality and community. At Gatherings, money is not the golden ticket that buys the very sustenance of living, but instead everyone is fed. Everyone can participate in some way that is valued, and it is not the responsibility of any one person or group to provide for the rest—rather it is the potential of all for all.

By seeing the congruence among material systems, ritual experience, forms of interaction, and broader social and cultural systems, we can begin to ask questions about how these systems work together in broader contexts and in mainstream society. This raises normative questions regarding the kinds of social systems we want to create and the technological systems that might help to get us there. Participation in the establishment and organization of the social world of a Rainbow Gathering is individually empowering and socially enhancing. Could mainstream society be reorganized to empower individuals and craft social collectivity through participation in the material means of sustenance and comfort?

The Challenge of Ritualized Freedom

This work demonstrates the constructed nature of social worlds and helps us recognize the crafted and social nature of our own worlds, which we may consider normal or outside the realm of social influence. Participation in social worlds—from Rainbow Gatherings to religious groups, sports teams, bowling leagues, and book clubs—involves interactions that come to shape how we view ourselves and others in the world around us.[14] A very key aspect to understanding social life is to recognize that different social worlds each involve a unique "scheme of life"[15]—socially contextual understandings of normal practice, social values, and rules guiding action and interaction. "The instincts and tendencies that find expression in any specific form of association are no doubt fundamentally human, but it is only under specific conditions that they assume the forms and exhibit the traits that are characteristic of any existing type."[16]

It is my hope that this presentation of Rainbow Gatherings, a study of "lives that otherwise go unnoticed"[17] in this unusual social world, will help you recognize the social nature of your own experiences and examine your own participation in various social worlds in a new light, as socially constructed and socially contextual rather than purely personal or practical. It is my hope that we can start to see ourselves "as whole human beings in a whole system."[18] After all, "social perspective and sanity of judgment come only from contact with social experience."[19]

Further, this work demonstrates that conflict and change are both inherent even in social worlds that seek to craft a heightened sense of social connectivity, and that conflict can actually work to reinforce collective effervescence, a useful insight for any group seeking to create coherence. Contradictions pose a threat to collective sentiments, yet also work to simultaneously enhance the sense of collectivity experienced at a Rainbow Gathering. This provides important insights into how collectivities are challenged and maintained.

One of the most interesting aspects of the Rainbow Gathering as a social world is that while most people participate in the culture and values of the Rainbow Family and most experience a sense of collective effervescence, certainly not everyone does. Rainbow Gatherings are free and open to all, and some of the people who come simply do not act or interact in "the Rainbow way." Some people just don't buy into the loving, open culture of Rainbow and do not act like they are connected to it.

One of the reasons that the Rainbow Family has been able to endure despite the presence of people and behaviors that contradict the culture and values is because those people and actions actually reinforce the feelings of collectivity for those who experience it. The people and things and actions that contradict the collective identity (be it alcohol, violence, nonparticipation, or people who simply don't feel the vibe) contribute to collective effervescence because at a Gathering, freedom and tolerance become more important than peace. This freedom means that individuals are free to act and interact in any way they choose, as long as their actions do not impinge upon the freedom of others to do the same. This freedom is also qualified by a respect for nature and a disavowal of physical violence, both of which are arguably about respecting the right of each individual to be free (free from environmental and physical harm).

Rainbow Gatherings are what philosopher John Stuart Mill called an "experiment in living"[20]—they are not perfect, they are not utopia; they are full of contradictions. Yet this ephemeral ritual event is an attempt to create a social world that embraces freedom in a robust sense, and social connection develops among individuals by embracing full freedom even in the face of contradictions and challenges. Respecting the freedom of others is an important part of what actually brings people together and unites them in feelings of collectivity. The contradictions that seemingly threaten communion also reinforce or contribute to it.

There are other groups that seem to strike this precarious balance making things that potentially threaten the sense of collectivity into a means of reinforcing it. For example, in the Amish community, teenagers are expected to leave their community for a period and must make their own choice to return. The Amish believe that becoming a child of God is an active choice that knowing adults must willingly make. Thus, even though sending their children away for a time presents a real potential threat to the continuation of their community, the process also reinforces their beliefs and their sense of collectivity.[21]

Alcoholics Anonymous and Narcotics Anonymous also arguably rest their sense of collectivity on this precarious ledge. Michael Niman writes that AA is the "only other long-lasting large nonhierarchical group operating under consensus rule . . . which, like the Family, is an 'occasional group.'"[22] The culture of these groups, reinforced by allowing anonymity, opposes the policing of individual behavior. Addicts can potentially continue to use and return to the group again and again. These groups' belief in human agency and the right to privacy potentially threaten their ability to keep addicts clean, but they reinforce the sense of collectivity and connection through shared and respected values.[23]

This is an important point for any group attempting to create and sustain a sense of connectivity and connection, an emotional attachment or sense of collective effervescence. Alternative communities in myriad forms as well as movements aimed at social change must grapple with how to embrace diversity and acceptance while also promoting cohesion and a sense of group identity. Issues, contradictions, and potential threats will inevitably arise. Successful groups are those for which these challenges are also means of reinforcing and sustaining group values and a sense of collectivity.

Yet the contradictory actions and people within the Rainbow Family pose the biggest challenge to the continued success of their Gatherings and have been increasing in prevalence over the forty-year lifetime of these events. Gender relations have always been a challenge to the Family, and they aren't necessarily moving toward more equality or respect. Some women are uncomfortable being alone at Gatherings; some men are disrespectful or downright predatory in their treatment of women and young girls.[24] The Internet makes it easier for people to find Gatherings, and so more people come for a greater diversity of reasons. Some younger people coming to Gatherings don't respect or participate in Rainbow culture. Many of them don't even make an audible noise during the Om circles.

At the 2012 Gathering, I heard the word "nigger," a word that many Americans today consider clearly disrespectful, more times than I care to remember, being shouted by some young (white) dirty kids who thought they were being funny or challenging status quo notions of appropriate speech. Some of the biggest questions facing the Family right now are related to how to deal with the increasing prevalence of words and deeds that do not correspond with Rainbow culture and how to continue embracing the freedom of all folks to come and gather even when they do not uphold many of the cultural values of the Gathering. As Butterfly Bill puts it, the dirty kids

> embrace even more the basic idea that the gathering is open to all people—no matter how crazy they seem at first, no matter what heavy problems they may be dealing with, no matter how abrasive their behavior can get to be—and greeting them with acceptance and support and opportunities to heal and grow. . . . They still want peace, which may be loud and raucous and filled with profanities at times, but still is a condition where nobody has to get what they want by fighting, and nobody gets injured or abused.
>
> With them, "The ideal of absolute openness is carried forth and made even more open. This is their interpretation of 'Welcome home.'"[25]

This, unfortunately, raises more questions than answers regarding the evolution and dissolution of the hippie counterculture and the challenges of cultural adaptation amid changing social contexts. In a generic and broad sense, ritual assembly "is the act by which society makes itself, and remakes itself, periodically."[26] The society being remade through the ritual of Rainbow Gatherings has changed throughout its history and inevitably will continue to change. As a Rainbow brother named Garrick put it, "We are witnessing a struggle between forces to expand our freedom, and forces to limit it. This is not necessarily between good and evil, but between more or less tolerance."[27] Profound social and cultural changes have taken place both inside the social world of Rainbow Gatherings and outside in the larger social worlds that impact Gathering culture. This social world, just like the other social worlds we inhabit, is shaped by and will continue to evolve in the face of demographic and cultural changes. Yet the core values guiding life at a Rainbow Gathering are not dead remnants of a dead countercultural movement; they are alive, they are emergent, and they continue to have the power to shape how we act, interact, and organize our social worlds.

Rainbow Gatherings as Experiments in Living

At the 2012 Gathering, I met a young man who called himself Mirror who had been traveling as a hobo musician with his girlfriend for six months before coming to the Gathering. Mirror described Rainbow Gatherings as "economic terrorism," using this phrase to describe why the Federal Bureau of Investigation supposedly has a file on the Rainbow Family (but apparently the Drug Enforcement Agency does not). For Mirror, "the Rainbow way" of providing everything necessary for free through voluntary engagement and active participation is a real threat to mainstream American society, materially, economically, and culturally. Can you imagine how significantly society would change if we began to organize our economies in "the Rainbow way," where everyone's needs were met regardless of financial or any other ability but where everyone was expected to somehow participate in what is required to meet those needs?

Certainly, the free provisions for thousands of gatherers are supplied temporarily and are dependent upon a whole lot of supplies and materials that are not free. Yet regardless of their source or cost, they are shared among all those who gather. You do not need the ability to pay; you do not need to even participate; you will still be fed. A free culture involves people interacting and sharing at a very localized and personal scale, and it can be adopted in all sorts of ways other than at a Gathering. Arguably, a localized economic culture (through support for local business, farmer's markets, and myriad other systems of sharing)[28] offers a more long-term and more widespread way to adopt some of the positive human experiences that flourish in Rainbow culture. Alternative currencies and time banks are two quickly expanding forms of unconventional accounting that allow people to trade their time for goods and services instead of relying on a traditional moneyed economy. Alternative communities are successful examples of how sharing systems can serve as the basis for reorganizing economic, material, and social systems in sustainable ways.[29]

Rainbow Gatherings present an active form of resistance to the dominant material and cultural systems in America. Although they may seem like nothing more than a deviant countercultural happening, deviance itself is only that which is defined as such,[30] and is always a vehicle for ideological struggles regarding what is considered socially legitimate.[31] At a Rainbow Gathering, money is not an accepted motivational currency or form of reward and everyone receives what they need regardless of their ability to purchase or produce it. In contrast to the systems of a Rainbow Gathering, the material systems that support life in mainstream society—indeed are necessary for life—are not open or transparent and are not participatory or freely provided. What does it say about us as a society, and what kind of society do we perpetuate, when our material systems are environmentally degrading and only available to those who can afford to pay for them? What kind of underlying cultural values shape our relationship to technology and to one another? What kind of orientations and practices would we rather see shaping our world and motivating our actions?

The emphasis placed on the value of freedom in Rainbow Gathering culture, as well as the values of both self-sufficiency and communal provisioning, certainly involves a form of patriotism. Many of the people who attend Rainbow Gatherings see themselves as true patriots. Many are veterans of war. While many demonstrate their political values through signs and stickers related to the Occupy movement, I also saw a handful of Ron Paul (a Republican politician and 2012 presidential hopeful) bumper stickers at the 2012 Gathering. Gatherings are events that uphold and protect the human freedom to freely gather on public land and to freely pursue individual understandings of liberty. These events can be viewed as experiments in living, as attempts at true liberty,[32] emphasizing human equality, active participation, and the rights of every individual to choose their own course of action and modes of interaction.

Yet these events also undo the bind between American ideals of freedom and American economic structures, presenting a countercultural version of patriotism. At the 2012 Gathering, I overheard an elder asking the Forest Service rangers why they didn't come to Gatherings as volunteers so that they could participate more freely and wouldn't have to charge the Federal Government for their time, since the Federal Government really can't afford to pay them overtime these days. At a Rainbow Gathering, capitalism is not patriotic. The pursuit of economic profit is not patriotic. Taking care of one another, materially and emotionally, is the only way to be truly patriotic, because it is the only way we can all be truly free.

This counterculture patriotism is about loving freedom even more than many self-identified American patriots do. I've had many Gathering participants tell me that they are indeed more patriotic than most. It is not a freedom to exploit or abuse. It is a freedom to act and interact as one chooses, but only if your freedom does not impose on the freedom of others and does not harm the sacred

Earth. It is also a freedom that does not involve economic exploitation or the pursuit of monetary profit. At the 2012 National Gathering, a sixty-six-year-old Vietnam veteran attendee said, "This is what America is all about. . . . We lead by example. We show the rest of the country what it can be like to be true human beings: We love one another, we respect one another, we show each other as much consideration and kindness as we can."[33]

This counterculture patriotism offers a means of embracing the best parts of many modern, democratic cultures (not just American culture) related to freedom, liberty, and human dignity while explicitly resisting any connection between capitalist economics and notions of human freedom. In many ways, "the Rainbow way" is also "the American way"—it is based on a strong work ethic, the value of active participation, and belief in the equality of all people. Perhaps it is even more American than modern American patriotism, because it detaches economic worth or ability to pay from human worth and ability to live. It recognizes both the sovereign autonomy of all beings and the inherent connections between all things. In doing so, this unusual social world provides importrant insight into how to rethink and reshape the material and cultural rituals of Babylon.

Being a Rainbow Sister
A Methodological Appendix

While I have attended six National Gatherings since 2002, I went to the 2012 National Rainbow Gathering for the explicit purpose of conducting fieldwork. I spent almost six weeks there, watching as this ephemeral social world emerged, evolved, and dissolved. During my time there, many choices and challenges arose, some of which I had prepared for and others that I did not expect.

There are so many things happening all the time at a Gathering, and it is impossible to be everywhere at once. I had to make choices, both before I arrived and throughout my time there, about how to best spend my time in order to learn as much as I could about Gathering culture and the material systems that support life in this world. One of the first choices that I made was to spend my time participating in and talking with people at many different kitchens rather than becoming more consistently involved with one particular kitchen. Many of the kitchens have their own distinct personalities and perspectives: Turtle Soup and Musical Veggie are quieter kitchens with many older folks and families; Jesus Kitchen, Home Shalom, and Krishna Kitchen have spiritual orientations that motivate participants and shape their activities; the crews at Montana Mud and Fat Kids are younger, louder, and rowdier. I wanted to spend my time learning about the diversity of perspectives and actions among the kitchens and attendees rather than getting a more in-depth look into the personalities and activities of one particular kitchen. However, there were differences in how kitchens reacted to my presence as a researcher. Montana Mud was incredibly welcoming, immediately allowing me to attend kitchen meetings and converse openly with highly involved individuals. For this, I thank them.

Given my particular interests in the material systems of Rainbow Gatherings and their relationship to the cultural system, as well as in the aspects of this event that make it a unique social world (specifically, shared language and practice), there are many facets of life at a Rainbow Gathering that I spent very little time learning about. While I attended some council meetings, I did not go to councils every day and I largely ignore all the many issues related to Rainbow governance here. Consensus-based decision-making processes and how they work out in actual practice are extremely fascinating and deserving of attention, but understanding Rainbow governance was not my intention here. Similarly, I did not examine the question of law enforcement with an eye toward conflict or structure—an issue that certainly could be studied at a Gathering. Michael Niman has attempted to document the structural and systematic campaign against the Rainbow Family by the FBI,[1] and Butterfly Bill describes the increasing interference of law enforcement at more recent Gatherings;[2] but, again, describing these aspects was not my purpose here. Instead, I chose to focus on the face-to-face interactions that actually occurred between rangers and gatherers in my presence.

I faced several challenges while conducting fieldwork. One that I didn't anticipate, although perhaps I should have based on past experiences at Gatherings, was related to gender. Men were much more willing to chat and share their experiences with me. Women often seemed like they didn't have the time or desire, and it sometimes felt as if men were willing to participate not out of interest in my work but as a part of their participation in the open sexual culture of the Gathering. Sometimes, their gazes or comments made me very uncomfortable and emotionally distracted me from the work I intended to do because my personal concerns became wrapped up in the gendered experience of a Gathering. However, my gender was an asset at times, as it made it possible for me to enter into conversations with male focalizers and facilitators who may have been less interested in talking to someone who wasn't young and female.[3]

The prevalence of Rainbow rumors and the general fuzziness of the truth at a Gathering were also quite challenging at times. Occasionally, I'd get comments that were completely unrelated to my questions. For instance, once I asked someone about a water filtration system and they responded by talking about the possibility of seeing Bigfoot. Sometimes, I'd hear contradictory information (sometimes even from the same person) or different pieces of a story that simply didn't add up. While the looseness of the truth and the acceptance of the fantastic contribute to the collective ritual of a Gathering, as a researcher it was sometimes very frustrating.

The separateness I experienced related to my privileged social position and differential *habitus* also posed a challenge to completely connecting with or being engulfed by Rainbow culture. I may in some ways "look the part." As of this writing, I myself have dreadlocks, and because I've attended many Gatherings and have a personal penchant for secondhand clothing, I wore attire appropriate for the setting. Yet many of my ways of acting, speaking, and carrying myself indicated a separateness or stranger-ness.[4] My vocabulary is different than that of many gatherers, and my behavior arguably more reserved (I have no interest, for example, in inserting capsulated powdered substances anally to get high, something that other gatherers were doing). A couple people commented on my cleanliness at this Gathering; as an eighteen-year-old, I was apparently more comfortable being dirty than I am today. Personal background and lifestyle choices, related to my educational and social position, set me apart from many of the gatherers I met.

Perhaps the biggest challenge for me personally was that, while conducting this kind of fieldwork, there is no time to get away, to take a break or pause from direct empirical experiences. Many ethnographic researchers spend years studying a particular group, yet while they might live near the group they study, they don't often live directly with the group. They spend time doing research, and they spend time at home, away from all that they are researching. This is not possible when doing research at a Gathering. I was at the Gathering from the beginning to the end, and every moment there challenged me to be aware, as a researcher, of my experiences and the inundation of information and personalities confronting me. Every conversation was potentially useful for research and thus required me to delicately introduce myself and my purpose at the Gathering, attempting to avoid deception while also continuing the conversation. I would wake in my sleep to the sounds of voices yelling (perhaps "We love you" or "nigger") and would then lie awake thinking about the yells and their social meaning. My first moments awake every morning, I could hear conversations happening around me and could not help but try to analyze them. It was, in many ways, exhausting.

Many of the Rainbow names used in this work are the names actually used by Gathering participants. I have met young Rainbow Gathering attendees who travel year-round named Skittles, Turtle, and Patches. Attend a National Rainbow Gathering, and you may meet Butterfly Bill, Tigger, and Roadrunner. I changed the names of some others, assigning pseudonym Rainbow names when I wanted to protect the identity of someone who worked closely with a particular kitchen, had not given direct permission for me to use their chosen Rainbow name, or had not been quoted in the newspaper in association with their Rainbow name.

This work is not intended to be a definitive account of the Rainbow Family or their Gatherings. No one person can speak for the Rainbow Family, and I am not attempting to speak for them here. I also cannot claim that this is the most truthful or real account of Gatherings possible; every gatherer has a different set of experiences that lead to varying understandings of what Gatherings are and what they offer. Here, I am only speaking as myself, and I am both Chelsea the Sociologist and Chelsea the Rainbow Sister. I can say only that I present the truth here as I have experienced it, organized by the analytical tools and perspectives offered by my education and profession, with an attempt to shed light on this unique social world that has meant so much to me can teach us about ourselves and the world around us.

A Glossary of Rainbow Gathering Vocabulary

A-camp: Located between the parking lot and Rainbow land, the physical location within the Rainbow Gathering where alcohol consumption is permitted and where gatherers who consume alcohol camp. Gatherers who camp in A-camp organize their own systems (kitchens, water provision, and shitters). Gatherers who camp in A-camp, who often overlap with the group who work the front gate, serve as the voluntary security force of the Gathering, ensuring that people coming to the Gathering with alcohol or with the intention of drinking alcohol stay in A-camp. A-campers are rougher, rowdier, and more violent than gatherers who camp in Rainbow land.

Babylo-meter: A watch or other time-keeping device; a tool of Babylon for measuring a constructed metric (time) that has no meaning or significance at a Gathering.

Babylon: How gatherers refer to the world outside the Gathering. According to longtime Rainbow Family participant Butterfly Bill, the term comes from a Bob Marley song quoting the 137th Psalm: "By the rivers of Babylon, where we sat down, and there we wept when we remembered Zion." In his memoir *Rainbow Gatherings*, Butterfly Bill writes, "Babylon was literally the place where the leaders of Judah were sent into exile. . . . Figuratively it was the decadent materialist world, and the things it did to your soul to keep you from realizing your true spiritual fulfillment" (68).

Bliss/bliss ware: The personal eating utensils that gatherers carry with them so that they can be served individual portions from the communal serving pots of food prepared by kitchens. This may include a bowl and/or plate; a spoon and/or fork; and a water bottle and/or drinking cup for hot beverages. There is a lot of variation in the kind, style, and quality of bliss ware carried by gatherers. Some gatherers carry forms of bliss sold by retail camping stores, often made of metal and with the clearly intended use of eating while on an outdoor adventure trip. Other gatherers use wooden bowls and spoons, plastic bowls carried in backpacks, or the cut-off bottoms of plastic jugs. Kitchens will often have extra makeshift bliss for gatherers who arrive without it.

Bliss ninny: A derogatory term for anyone who is lazy, unhelpful, or so "blissed out" that they do not participate in any of the work necessary to sustain a Gathering.

Bliss pit: A fire pit intended for gathering around, as opposed to cooking over. Kitchens typically have cooking fires and separate bliss pits.

Bliss rail: A shelf made from tree branches lashed together between two trees to make a shelf. Located at the front of a kitchen, the bliss rail is used to serve food during communal meals. It is also where water is made available, in a water buffalo that is set atop the bliss rail for self-service. The bliss rail also helps to keep kitchen spaces slightly closed off so that gatherers don't unknowingly wander through space intended for food preparation and open only to kitchen crew.

Boogie pit: A larger fire pit intended for drum circles, where multiple drummers play together while others dance and sometimes sing or chant around them. Boogie pits are often located away from any one particular kitchen, centrally located in between multiple kitchens. Boogie pits are also referred to as bliss pits, although bliss pits are not referred to as boogie pits.

Brother: A common term of identification for male Rainbow gatherers.

Busket: The buckets, typically large metal coffee containers, that gatherers associated with Nic at Night carry around with them, containing the smoking supplies they've acquired by yelling their hallmark phrase, "Need a cigarette, we got a cigarette, got a cigarette, we need a cigarette!" Most typically, buskets contain loose rolling tobacco and papers. "Tailor mades" (filtered cigarettes sold in packs) are considered by many to be a luxury commodity at Gatherings, although other gatherers conscientiously avoid them.

Circle: Used in reference to the Gathering's nightly dinner meal. It's sometimes used alone, as in when someone asks if you're "going to circle" or when gatherers yell "Circle!" to let others know that it's time to gather for dinner. Gatherers also refer to "main circle" (used for both the main circle nightly meal, which is also referred to as "dinner circle," and the afternoon events of July 4) and "Om circle" (the practice of holding hands to Om together, which takes place prior to every main circle meal as well as on July 4).

Clean-up crew: The group of self-identifying volunteers who stay on site after July 4 and take an active role in cleaning up the Gathering site.

Council: A generic term referencing the consensus-based decision-making bodies of the Rainbow Gathering. There are many different forms of council, including a daily council (a meeting that takes place at noon every day to discuss and resolve issues), a banking council (the group that is entrusted to collect, account for, and distribute funds from the Magic Hat), kitchen council (a group that meets to discuss issues affecting all kitchens and to coordinate the main circle meal), and clean-up council (meetings among clean-up crew). Vision Council, where locations for the next year's Gathering are discussed and a decision is made about a specific state, group of states, or region to explore for the next annual event, is the most official (beginning at noon on July 7) and longest lasting (often taking place from noon until "it's too dark to see one another's eyes" over several consecutive days). Spring council is a meeting among the scouts who have been looking for the next National Gathering site to decide on the specific site; this council takes place each spring immediately prior to the announcement of the site for the National Gathering. All councils are open to all interested participants.

Dark thirty: Nighttime.

Disappear/disappeared/disappearing: A way to describe the work that clean-up crew does to eliminate all evidence of human presence in the National Forest. Fire pits, compost pits, and shitters are filled in; kitchens are completely dismantled and the wood used for construction is scattered; and all trash is removed from the site. These are examples of disappearing, all inspired by the leave-no-trace, earth-wise responsible freedom ethic of Rainbow Gathering culture. To further disappear the Gathering, trails and meadows are reseeded with appropriate seed, as indicated by the Forest Service.

Doser (mad doser): A person who freely provides "doses" (drugs, most often hallucinogens) to a large number of people.

Downtown: The central area in Rainbow land.

Drainbow: Someone who does not participate in the material or cultural systems of a Rainbow Gathering. Instead of contributing, they drain both material and energetic resources without giving anything back to the community.

Drum circle: Where multiple drummers play together. Nightly drum circles at Rainbow Gatherings are common and often quite large and loud.

Flying a sign/flying signs: When people hold up signs (such as "anything helps") as a means of asking for donations, typically money or food. Although many full-time travelers who attend Gatherings are experienced sign flyers, having often used this method of requesting alms while traveling, flying signs is discouraged at a Rainbow Gathering or in the local community near the Rainbow Gathering site.

Front gate: The area in the parking lot where people are welcomed home, given parking instructions, and walk into the Gathering; where the main trail meets the parking lot.

Ganja: Marijuana.

Heart song: What someone shares when it is their turn to speak during a council meeting, particularly during Vision Council. Councils typically involve passing a feather or some other object around the circle; each person is invited to speak (share their heart song) when it's their turn to hold the object. Heart songs vary widely, from brief ("I'm so glad to be here" or "Lovin' you, family") to very verbose (a story about a past Gathering) and from directly on topic (opinions about potential future Gathering sites) to meandering and emotional (thoughts about the future of the Earth and humankind).

Hi holies: A term, sometimes used derogatorily, to refer to elders who are or who see themselves as integrally involved in facilitating and focalizing roles at the Gathering.

Information/information booth: A table set up at every National Gathering where people can find information, including but not limited to the mini-manual (introductory guide to Rainbow Gatherings); *All Ways Free* (the annual Gathering newsletter); a ride share/lost and found/people-finding board where anyone is free to post a note about anything; and an ever-evolving map of the Gathering.

Jugging: Asking strangers to pay for gasoline; involves parking at a gas station and approaching people while they are filling up.

Kick down (verb) and kick-downs (noun): Things gifted to individuals or kitchens.

Kitchen crew: The group of people who voluntarily participate in the organization and day-to-day tasks of a particular kitchen.

Lovin' you: A phrase commonly exchanged between individuals and among groups at Gatherings.

Magic Hat: All monetary donations made to purchase provisions for Main Supply are made to the Magic Hat. During the nightly main circle meal, a group of volunteers (often associated with the banking council) will carry a bucket or hat around the circle and serenade eaters with impromptu tunes about the importance of donating to the Magic Hat. Donations to the Magic Hat can also be made at the information booth anytime. Donations to the Magic Hat are the only acceptable way of using monetary currency at a Gathering.

Main circle: The dinner circle and the main circle that takes place on July 4.

Main meadow: A large meadow where main circle/dinner circle (the nightly meal) and the July 4 celebrations take place.

Main Supply: The stock of provisions attained and distributed during the Rainbow Gathering. Main Supply involves daily runs in a big truck or school bus to pick up massive amounts of bulk food items, which are then distributed to all kitchens serving main circle as well as to Kid Village.

Mama: A common term of identification for female Rainbow gatherers.

Mini-manual: An introductory guide to Rainbow Gatherings, available at Information.

Movie: An activity. For instance, a kitchen might have a "zu zu movie at dark thirty"—meaning that they will be making and serving something sweet at night. Movie might also be used as in "that's their movie"—meaning that's what that individual is doing or is into at the moment.

Nic at Night: The group of gatherers who voluntarily carry around and distribute free tobacco products.

Om: The sacred syllable of Hinduism. The breathing of "om" (rhymes with "home") connects many breaths into one. There is an Om circle where gatherers stand, hold hands, and collectively chant om at the beginning of every main circle meal and at Rainbow noon on July 4 to initiate the day of celebration.

Parking lot: Where people park their cars, whether an actual lot or simply along a road. Alcohol consumption is permitted in the parking lot.

Procrastination station: An either organized or impromptu spot along a main trail where gatherers stop to chat, smoke cigarettes or marijuana, share snacks, or otherwise delay proceeding on their intended journey.

Rap: An informal speech. There are two particularly important raps in Rainbow Gathering culture. Rap 107 is about Gathering consciousness, providing an overview of the culture and expectations of practice at a Gathering. Rap 701, which starts "pack it in—pack it out!" is about the leave-no-trace ethic.

Rainbow land: Where the Gathering takes place, excluding the parking lot, front gate, and A-camp.

Rainbow name: A chosen name used at a Gathering, in contrast to the given "slave name" used in Babylon. Some full-time travelers eschew given names altogether and are always referred to using a chosen name like Tigger, Patches, Turtle, or Skittles.

Rainbow noon: A loose time reference; when the sun is high in the sky.

Rainbow rumors: Fantastical tales and other false information that spreads around a Gathering. The most common Rainbow rumor is cancellation (that the National Gathering is not going to happen).

Rainbow way: Helpful voluntary participation in multiple forms that benefits the community—from hauling supplies like food and water to picking up trash to offering to wash dishes after a communal meal.

Road block: In its positive usage, this refers to instances when a group of gatherers sit alongside or sometimes in the middle of the trail, blocking the way and inviting passersby to join in a friendly conversation, a break for a cigarette, or a communal marijuana smoking session. Rainbow Gathering participants are also familiar with this term in its negative usage, as police or Forest Service rangers will sometimes set up road blocks on roads leading into a Rainbow Gathering to check identification and vehicle registration or search cars.

Seven up: Rainbow Gathering vocabulary for Forest Service rangers, which gatherers yell whenever rangers are visible to warn others of their presence.

Shanti Sena: The voluntary peacekeepers of the Gathering who use loving language and nonviolent means to diffuse negative interactions. When a confrontation or an episode of violence arises, gatherers yell "Shanti Sena!" and anyone who considers themselves part of this voluntary group will come to the scene and attempt to resolve the issue through peaceful means.

Shitter: Communal trench latrines constructed and utilized by gatherers. These always involve a long, narrow trench dug into the ground accompanied by a waterproof canister holding toilet paper, a second containing ash or lime, and a third made to dispense a bleach-water hand wash. Shitters are constructed and maintained in association with particular kitchens, and some kitchen crews modify theirs to enhance comfort, adding features like boxes with toilet seats and privacy curtains.

Shitter digger: Someone who voluntarily digs shitters.

Sister: A common term of identification for female Rainbow gatherers.

Six up: Rainbow Gathering vocabulary for law enforcement officers who carry guns, which gatherers yell whenever officers are visible to warn others of their presence.

Tradeables: Goods like clothing, candy bars, cold sodas, pretty rocks, camping supplies, artwork, musical instruments, and illicit substances like marijuana or psychedelic mushrooms that are traded in trade circle.

Trade circle: The bartering system of the Gathering, where people sit behind blankets covered with their tradeables and trade with one another and passersby. Money is not an accepted form of currency. Trade circles used to be spatially organized as actual circles off of a main trail; at more recent Gatherings, traders have set up in a long line right along the main trail.

Water buffalo: A large container of filtered water made available to all gatherers.

Weekend warrior: A somewhat derogatory term for gatherers who take a break from conventional lives in Babylon to attend Rainbow Gatherings, perhaps attending for the weekend, but who do not actively participate in the organizational, physical, or energetic work necessary to support life at a Gathering.

Welcome home: A phrase commonly exchanged between individuals and among groups at Gatherings.

Zu zu: A categorical term for all kinds of sweets and treats like chocolate, cake, and candy bars.

NOTES

Notes for Introduction

1. Michael Niman, *People of the Rainbow: A Nomadic Utopia*, 2nd ed. (Knoxville: University of Tennessee Press, 2011), 98. See also Alan G. Fix, "Fission-Fusion and Lineal Effect: Aspects of the Population Structure of the Semai Senoi of Malaysia," *American Journal of Physical Anthropology* 43 (1975): 295–302.

2. Niman, *People of the Rainbow*, xvii.

3. Ibid.

4. Ibid.

5. This is sometimes restricted in actual usage, in Rainbow pamphlets and conversations, to "every non-violent human with a belly-button."

6. On the concept of social world and particular studies of social worlds, see Paul G. Cressey, *The Taxi-Dance Hall: A Sociological Study in Commercialized Recreation and City Life* (Chicago: University of Chicago Press, 1932); Nels Anderson, *The Hobo* (Chicago: University of Chicago Press, 1961 [1923]); Paul S. P. Siu, *The Chinese Laundryman: A Study of Social Isolation* (New York: New York University Press, 1987).

7. Patricia A. Adler and Peter Adler, *Constructions of Deviance: Power, Context, and Interaction*, 5th ed. (Belmont, CA: Thomson Wadsworth, 2006), 1.

8. Howard Becker, *Outsiders: Studies in the Sociology of Deviance* (New York: Free Press, 1991 [1963]), 178. Becker claims that sociology is the study of "collective action," 182.

9. Ibid., 181.

10. Sociologist David Unruh defines a social world "as a unit of social organization which is diffuse and amorphous in character. Generally larger than groups or organizations, social worlds are not necessarily defined by formal boundaries, membership lists,

or spatial territory." He goes on to write, "a social world must be seen as an internally recognizable constellation of actors, organizations, events, and practices which have coalesced into a perceived sphere of interest and involvement for participants." David Unruh, "Characteristics and Types of Participation in Social Worlds," *Symbolic Interaction* 2 (1979): 115–130, 115.

11. Cressey, *The Taxi-Dance Hall*.

12. Siu, *The Chinese Laundryman*.

13. Anselm Strauss, "A Social World Perspective," in *Creating Sociological Awareness*, ed. A. Strauss (New Brunswick, NJ: Transaction Press, 1990 [1978]), 233–244, 236.

14. Cressey, *The Taxi-Dance Hall*, 31.

15. Andrew Abbott, *Department and Discipline: Chicago Sociology at One Hundred* (Chicago: University of Chicago Press, 1999), 399.

16. Ibid., 6.

17. Butterfly Bill [William S. Hirsch], *Rainbow Gatherings: A Memoir* (Muskogee, OK: Bliss Fire Press, 2010).

18. Marcel Mauss, *Seasonal Variations of the Eskimo: A Study in Social Morphology* (London: Routledge and Kegan Paul, 1979).

19. Emile Durkheim, *Elementary Forms of Religious Life* (New York: The Free Press, 1995 [1912]); Mauss, *Seasonal Variations of the Eskimo*; Randall Collins, *Interaction Ritual Chains* (Princeton, NJ: Princeton University Press, 2004).

20. Butterfly Bill, *Rainbow Gatherings*.

21. Mauss, *Seasonal Variations of the Eskimo*, 19.

22. Emile Durkheim in *L'Annee sociologique*, vol. 2, 1899, p. 520. Cited in James Fox's translator's foreword to Mauss, *Seasonal Variations of the Eskimo*, 3.

23. Mauss, *Seasonal Variations of the Eskimo*, 20.

24. Victor Turner, *The Ritual Process* (London: Routledge and Kegan Paul, 1969).

25. Collins, *Interaction Ritual Chains*.

26. See Mustafa Emirbayer, "Durkheim's Contribution to the Sociological Analysis of History," *Sociological Forum* 11 (1996): 263–284.

27. Georg Simmel, "The Problem of Sociology," in *Georg Simmel: On Individuality and Social Forms*, ed. Donald N. Levine (Chicago: University of Chicago Press, 1971), 23–34; Georg Simmel, "Sociability: An Example of Pure, or Formal, Sociology," in *The Sociology of Georg Simmel*, ed. and trans. Kurt H. Wolff (New York: The Free Press, 1950), 39–57.

28. Sociologists often recognize commonalities between Erving Goffman and Georg Simmel. For instance, "Goffman is also famous for not being a 'systematic' theoretician. His fame, perhaps like Simmel's to whom he is often compared, is as a descriptive theoretician of the episodic." Bradley H. Brewster and Michael Mayerfeld Bell, "The Environmental Goffman: Toward an Environmental Sociology of Everyday Life," *Society and Natural Resources* 23 (2010): 45–57, 47.

29. Erving Goffman, *Interaction Ritual: Essays on Face-to-Face Behavior* (New York: Pantheon, 1967), Introduction.

30. Georg Simmel, "The Field of Sociology," in *The Sociology of Georg Simmel,* ed. and trans. Kurt H. Wolff (New York: The Free Press, 1950), 3–25; Simmel, "The Problem of Sociology."

31. Simmel, "Sociability," 40.

32. There is one other academic book about Rainbow Gatherings that I'm aware of: Michael Niman's *People of the Rainbow: A Nomadic Utopia.* I would argue that his book is more comprehensive but less conceptually driven than this one. He covers some of the things that I don't, like the structural conflicts in the relationship between law enforcement (from local police and Forest Service to the FBI) and the Rainbow Family. However, he is not a sociologist, and thus he doesn't put forth a particular sociological case in his writing. Relying on a perspective influenced by the approach to social worlds taken by sociologists in the Chicago School, as well as by the examination of material culture and cultural ritual prevalent in the work of sociologists Emile Durkheim and Marcel Mauss, my goal is not only to interestingly present this unique group and their happenings to the reader, but also to make a sociological argument that teaches us about our interaction with the world more broadly. Other books about Rainbow Gatherings include David Sentelle, *Judge David and the Rainbow People* (Washington, DC: Green Bag Press, 2002); Mary Kohut, *Welcome Home: A Look into the Rainbow Family of the Living Light* (self-published, 2008); Butterfly Bill, *Rainbow Gatherings*; Butterfly Bill, *Volume Two: 2000–2012* (Muskogee, OK: Bliss Fire Press, 2013). Butterfly Bill's ethnographic reviews of almost three decades of Rainbow Gatherings provide much valuable insight and I refer to him often herein.

33. Mauss, *Seasonal Variations of the Eskimo.*

34. Georg Simmel, "The Metropolis and Mental Life," in *Georg Simmel: On Individuality and Social Forms,* ed. Donald N. Levine (Chicago: University of Chicago Press, 1971), 324–335.

35. Goffman, *Interaction Ritual*; see also Collins, *Interaction Ritual Chains.*

36. Randall Collins, "From 'Stratification, Emotional Energy, and the Transient Emotions,'" in *Emile Durkheim: Sociologist of Modernity,* ed. Mustafa Emirbayer (Oxford: Blackwell Publishers, 2003), 129–133.

37. Unruh, "Characteristics and Types of Participation in Social Worlds," 124.

38. Becker, *Outsiders,* 204.

39. John Stuart Mill, *On Liberty* (Boston: Ticknor and Fields, 1863).

40. See Pierre Bourdieu, *The Logic of Practice* (Stanford: Stanford University Press, 1990); Pierre Bourdieu and Loic J. D. Wacquant, *An Invitation to Reflexive Sociology* (Chicago: University of Chicago Press, 1992).

41. Georg Simmel, "The Stranger," in *Classical Sociological Theory,* 2nd ed., ed. Craig Calhoun et al. (West Sussex, UK: Wiley-Blackwell, 2007), 295–299.

42. According to David Unruh, "strangers are full-fledged members of a group simply because they are positioned outside and confront the group simultaneously." "Characteristics and Types of Participation in Social Worlds," 116.

43. Simmel, "The Stranger," 297.

44. Sociologist Pierre Bourdieu uses the word *habitus* to mean "a system of lasting dispositions which, integrating past experiences, functions at every moment as a matrix of perceptions, appreciations and actions." Each individual person occupies and acts within a particular habitus, which "could be considered as a subjective but not individual system of internalized structures, schemes of perception, conception, and action common to all members of the same group or class." See Pierre Bourdieu, *Outline of a Theory of Practice* (Cambridge: Cambridge University Press, 1977), 82–83, 86. See also Pierre Bourdieu, "Social Space and Symbolic Space," and Pierre Bourdieu, "Structures, *Habitus*, Practices," in *Contemporary Sociological Theory*, 2nd ed., ed. Craig Calhoun et al. (West Sussex, UK: Wiley-Blackwell, 2007), pp. 259–289.

45. Erving Goffman, *The Presentation of Self in Everyday Life* (New York: Overlook Press, 1959), 25.

46. Durkheim, *Elementary Forms of Religious Life*, 14–15.

47. Some of my favorite ethnographies were written by authors from the Chicago School, like Paul Cressey's *The Taxi-Dance Hall* and Nels Anderson's *The Hobo*. More recent ethnographies that have inspired me, methodologically although not necessarily topically or theoretically, include Terry Williams, *Crackhouse: Notes from the End of the Line* (Reading, MA: Addison-Wesley Publishing, 1992); Philippe Bourgois, *In Search of Respect: Selling Crack in El Barrio* (Cambridge: Cambridge University Press, 2003); Jay MacLeod, *Ain't No Making It: Aspirations and Attainment in a Low-Income Neighborhood* (Boulder, CO: Westview Press, 2009); and Matthew Desmond, *On the Fireline: Living and Dying with Wildland Firefighters* (Chicago: University of Chicago Press, 2007). Like Desmond and MacLeod, I became involved in the social world I study years before bringing along a notebook and officially researching my surroundings. Like Williams and Bourgois, I study a social world that is unfamiliar to most people. Like all of these authors, I attempt to weave the direct experience, words, and thoughts of those in the world I study, including myself, with an analysis of that world.

48. William S. Hirsch, known by his Rainbow name Butterfly Bill, self-published his memoirs, which share his accounts of being introduced to the Rainbow Family and becoming involved in the organizational tasks and focalizing roles that make Gatherings happen. While I do not agree with all of the opinions he shares in his work, I wouldn't expect to, because everybody's Gathering experience is different and no one speaks or can speak for the Rainbow Family. His stories serve as historical reference and reaffirmations of (as well as challenges to) my own experiences, providing quality data and enriching stories to add to and reshape my own. See Butterfly Bill, *Rainbow Gatherings: A Memoir*, and Butterfly Bill, *Volume Two*.

49. See, for example, Desmond, *On the Fireline*.

Notes for Chapter 1

1. See Michael Niman, *People of the Rainbow: A Nomadic Utopia,* 2nd ed. (Knoxville: University of Tennessee Press, 2011); Butterfly Bill [William S. Hirsch], *Rainbow Gatherings: A Memoir* (Muskogee, OK: Bliss Fire Press, 2010); and http://welcomehome.org/rainbow/index.html for more on the historical beginnings of Rainbow Gatherings.

2. Michael Niman writes, "The peace activists promoted peace, while the veterans were sick of violence. It was a natural union. The veterans, using skills learned in Vietnam, created much of the Gatherings' infrastructure, from "MASH/CALM" medical facilities to field kitchens and latrines. The confluence of these two groups working, living, and loving together, was part of a national healing process when American involvement in the Vietnam war ended. Where "hippies" and construction workers squared off in the 1960s, peace activists and veteran warriors started building a new society in the 1970s and 1980s. The combination gives the Family a strength that many Rainbows feel it would never have had otherwise." *People of the Rainbow,* 34.

3. Anthony Ripley, "Peace and Religious Festival Begins in Colorado," *New York Times,* July 2, 1972.

4. In this way, Rainbow Gatherings are similar to the winter culture of ritual and connectivity among Eskimos described by Marcel Mauss in *Seasonal Variations of the Eskimo.* Like when the Eskimo are gathered for collective winter life, there is no system of formal punishment at a Rainbow Gathering, only moral sanction through praise or public shaming of sorts. It is, "therefore, a marvelous example of the Arab definition of a clan: *the place where there is no blood vengeance. Even public crimes are* generally the object of only moral punishment." Marcel Mauss, *Seasonal Variations of the Eskimo: A Study in Social Morphology* (London: Routledge and Kegan Paul, 1979), 67, italics in original. As Butterfly Bill puts it, "There were no arrests, trials, sentences, or jails, you couldn't fire anybody, it was only the possible fear of negative public opinion that could be a deterrent to anyone." *Rainbow Gatherings,* 217–218.

5. Nels Anderson, *The Hobo* (Chicago: University of Chicago Press, 1961 [1923]).

6. Butterfly Bill has this to say about the Rainbow vocabulary word "Babylon": "This meant the world outside of the gathering. . . . It was introduced to the Family by gatherers who were into the reggae music of Bob Marley, who was a Rastafarian and used the language of that faith in the lyrics of his songs. One of his songs quoted the 137th Psalm: *'By the rivers of Babylon, where we sat down, and there we wept when we remembered Zion.'* Babylon was literally the place where the leaders of Judah were sent into exile, as described in the final chapters of the second books of Kings and Chronicles, many parts of Jeremiah, and all of Daniel in the Bible. Figuratively it was the decadent materialist world, and the things it did to your soul to keep you from realizing your true spiritual fulfillment." Butterfly Bill, *Rainbow Gatherings,* 68.

7. Butterfly Bill, *Rainbow Gatherings,* 82.

8. See William Cronon, "The Trouble with Wilderness: Or, Getting Back to the

Wrong Nature," in *Uncommon Ground: Rethinking the Human Place in Nature,* ed. W. Cronon (New York: Norton, 1996), 69–90.

9. A complete list of past Rainbow Gathering sites is available at http://welcomehome .org/rainbow/index.html, under "Historical Stuff." Accessed October 8, 2012.

10. Butterfly Bill, *Rainbow Gatherings,* 67.

11. A longtime participant in Rainbow Gatherings, a man who calls himself Tigger, said, "'The primary starters of the Rainbow Gathering were combat veterans from Vietnam along with a bunch of peace-loving hippies,' explaining that, today as then, many veterans returning from war have trouble fitting back into society." Quoted in Debra Mccown, "Rainbow Gathering Draws People from All 'Walks and Colors,'" last modified June 18, 2012, http://www2.tricities.com/news/2012/jun/18/rainbow -gathering-draws-people-all-walks-and-color-ar-1994743/, accessed October 11, 2012.

12. See http://welcomehome.org/rainbow/index.html.

13. See http://bliss-fire.com/.

14. In an Om circle, people stand, join hands, and "soon the long drawn out O vowel" fills the air with sound. In an Om circle, people are chanting "Om"—"pronounced to rhyme with 'home,' the sacred syllable of Hinduism." Butterfly Bill, *Rainbow Gatherings,* 30.

15. Butterfly Bill, *Rainbow Gatherings,* 41.

16. In this section, I compile memories from several National Gatherings to share events that are all true, but aggregated to create a composite story. Niman's *People of the Rainbow* includes a similar narrative intended to introduce readers to Rainbow Gatherings.

17. Kitchens serve exclusively vegetarian and mostly vegan food at the main circle dinner meal, and they let everyone know if their food contains dairy. I believe this is about cultural values related to the land and animals as well as practical considerations regarding providing food for people with diverse dietary and lifestyle choices and feeding many people on a limited budget.

18. Emile Durkheim, *Elementary Forms of Religious Life* (New York: Free Press, 1995 [1912]), 217–218.

19. *USA v. Adams,* Great Falls, Montana, November 15, 2000. CR-00-5037-GF -RFC. Cited in Butterfly Bill, *Rainbow Gatherings,* 307.

20. Durkheim, *Elementary Forms of Religious Life.*

21. Ibid.

22. Ibid.

23. Chris Shilling, "Embodiment, Experience and Theory: In Defence of the Sociological Tradition," *The Sociological Review* 49 (2001): 327–344, 335.

24. Experiencing the heightened social energy and connectivity of collective effervescence can "generate 'a sort of electricity' which launches people to an 'extraordinary' state of 'exaltation.'" Shilling, "Embodiment, Experience and Theory," 335. Shilling cites Durkheim, *Elementary Forms of Religious Life,* 213, 217.

25. Mauss, *Seasonal Variations of the Eskimo*, 58.

26. Shilling, "Embodiment, Experience and Theory," 335. Shilling cites Emile Durkheim, "The Dualism of Human Nature and Its Social Conditions," in *Emile Durkheim on Morality and Society*, ed. R. N. Bellah (Chicago: University of Chicago Press, 1973 [1914]).

27. Victor Turner, *The Ritual Process* (London: Routledge and Kegan Paul, 1969), 97, 126–129.

28. Ibid., 129. On the similarities between Emile Durkheim and Victor Turner, see Tim Olaveson, "Collective Effervescence and Communitas: Processual Models of Ritual and Society in Emile Durkheim and Victor Turner," *Dialectical Anthropology* 26 (2001): 89–124.

29. Turner, *The Ritual Process*, 138.

30. Randall Collins, *Interaction Ritual Chains* (Princeton, NJ: Princeton University Press, 2004).

31. Ibid.

32. See John Stuart Mill, *On Liberty* (Boston: Ticknor and Fields, 1863).

Notes for Chapter 2

1. Most people at Rainbow Gatherings go by a Rainbow name, such as Tigger or Plunker or Hugger or Skittles, and do not use their "Babylonian" or given name (which I've also heard referred to as "slave name") at all. This, of course, contributes to the sense of freedom and celebration at a Gathering, where anyone can be anything they want to be, including Dancing Bear, Karma, or Shipwreck.

2. Forest Service regulations forbid rangers from accepting any food or drink from gatherers.

3. Code of Federal Regulations, Title 36, Land Uses and Prohibitions, Final Rule, 1995. Cited in Butterfly Bill [William S. Hirsch], *Rainbow Gatherings: A Memoir* (Muskogee, OK: Bliss Fire Press, 2010), 226.

4. This chapter is modeled after Chapter 6 in Paul Cressey's *The Taxi-Dance Hall*, which presents ideal-typical categorizations of the types of patron who frequent the dance hall. Paul G. Cressey, *The Taxi-Dance Hall: A Sociological Study in Commercialized Recreation and City Life* (Chicago: University of Chicago Press, 1932).

5. Also based on my own experience, I would guess that the racial composition of most Gatherings is unfortunately pretty similar to the very white town of Madison, Wisconsin, where I lived for several years while completing my formal education.

6. Of course, all of the people at Rainbow spend at least some of their lives in Babylon, so these issues don't completely disappear.

7. Butterfly Bill, *Rainbow Gatherings*, 169–170.

8. According to Butterfly Bill, the Forest Service's method of estimating attendance at a Gathering is to count cars. He is not convinced of this method's reliability, nor am I; it would be impossible to predict how many people arrive in each car, as many people hitchhike or find other means of getting to Gatherings without personal transportation. Butterfly Bill [William S. Hirsch], *Rainbow Gatherings, Volume Two: 2000–2012* (Muskogee, OK: Bliss Fire Press, 2013), 101.

9. Similar to the days recounted in Nels Anderson's *The Hobo* (Chicago: University of Chicago Press, 1961 [1923]). Hitchhikers, trainhoppers, temporary workers, and wanderers of all kinds are still here in America. Perhaps we as a culture have just worked harder to forget, ignore, or otherwise "disappear" them.

10. Quoted in Debra Mccown, "Rainbow Gathering Draws People from All 'Walks and Colors,'" http://www2.tricities.com/news/2012/jun/18/rainbow-gathering -draws-people-all-walks-and-color-ar-1994743/, June 18, 2012.

11. Tim Cahill, "Granby, Colorado, 1972: Armageddon Postponed," *Rolling Stone,* August 3, 1972.

12. See Robert M. Bossarte et al., "Injury, Violence, and Risk among Participants in a Mass Gathering of the Rainbow Family of Living Light," *Journal of Health Care for the Poor and Underserved* 19 (2008): 588–595, 592.

13. See http://fatkidskitchen.wordpress.com/, accessed January 22, 2014.

14. Trade circles have changed over the forty-year history of Gatherings, with both the centrality of trade and the voraciousness with which people trade increasing substantially. Trade is a contentious issue within the Family. Perhaps "trader" could even be another category of Rainbow participant, as some people aggressively hawk their wares and spend their days entirely focused on trade, interacting with other Gathering participants based on their categorization as a trader.

15. Quoted in Rain Smith, "More Than 10,000 Hippies Expected in Cherokee Forest by July Fourth," *Kingsport Times-News*, June 20, 2012, http://www.timesnews.net /article/9048205/more-than-10000-hippies-expected-in-cherokee-forest-by-july-fourth, accessed October 11, 2012.

16. Michael Niman, *People of the Rainbow: A Nomadic Utopia,* 2nd ed. (Knoxville: University of Tennessee Press, 2011), 37.

17. There are even terms to describe those who live fairly mainstream or monetarily comfortable lives but still hold on to their countercultural values: they are called "house hippies" and sometimes "trustafarians."

18. Butterfly Bill, *Rainbow Gatherings, Volume Two,* 132.

19. See Butterfly Bill's chapter on the 2012 National Gathering in ibid.

20. See "raps" and the "mini-manual" at http://welcomehome.org/rainbow/index .html, accessed December 19, 2013. The mini-manual provided at the 1995 Annual Rainbow Gathering is reprinted in Butterfly Bill's *Rainbow Gatherings,* 356–360.

21. Butterfly Bill, *Rainbow Gatherings.*

22. Perhaps because they occur in remote locations usually surrounded only by small rural towns, National Rainbow Gatherings receive quite a bit of local press while they're occurring through local articles, often with colorful titles. See, for example, Debra Mccown, "Rainbow Gathering Draws People from All 'Walks and Colors'"; Rain Smith, "More Than 10,000 Hippies Expected in Cherokee Forest by July Fourth"; Allie Robinson, "Many of the Rainbowers Are Professionals Who Just Come to Get Away," *Bristol Herald Courier* (Virginia), June 24, 2012; "Rainbow Festival Has Its Positives," http://www2.tricities.com/news/2012/jun/27/rainbow-festival-has-its-positives-ar-2015963/, June 27, 2012, accessed October 11, 2012; Nate Morabito, "Public Nudity an Issue during Rainbow Family Gathering," http://www2.wjhl.com/news/2012/jul/06/public-nudity-issue-during-rainbow-family-gatherin-ar-2039115/, July 6, 2012, accessed October 11, 2012; Allie Robinson, "Texas Tim: 'I Was Brought up Leaving the Place Better Than You Found It,'" http://www2.tricities.com/news/2012/jul/15/texas-tim-i-was-brought-leaving-place-better-you-f-ar-2057552/, July 15, 2012, accessed October 11, 2012; Roger Brown, "Rainbow Gathering Area in the Cherokee National Forest Almost Back to Normal," http://www2.tricities.com/news/2012/jul/31/rainbow-gathering-area-cherokee-national-forest-al-ar-2096192/, July 31, 2012, accessed October 11, 2012.

23. Some locals seem to come exclusively for this reason. They are often identifiable on weekend nights, more enthusiastic or intoxicated than other participants. Walking the trail, you'll hear many locals talking with one another about their wild and crazy times in the woods.

24. Locals are like social world tourists, whom David Unruh characterizes as wanting to experience what is perceived to be the essence of the social world. "Characteristics and Types of Participation in Social Worlds," *Symbolic Interaction* 2 (1979): 115–130, 118–119.

25. Pronounced *shahn-tih-SEE-nuh*, these words reportedly mean "peace army" in Sanskrit. Butterfly Bill, *Rainbow Gatherings*, 44.

26. Mostly, interactions with Forest Service rangers are pleasant. They get to know the faces and the personalities at the Gathering, especially through their conversations with focalizers and facilitators. Many of the rangers come to wave and say hello when driving through the parking lot; I've heard stories of rangers coming back in plainclothes to enjoy the Gathering after work.

27. Butterfly Bill, *Rainbow Gatherings*, 55.

28. See Butterfly Bill's chapter on the 2012 National Gathering in Butterfly Bill, *Rainbow Gatherings, Volume Two*.

29. This generational shift may also start to shift some of the general character of Gatherings, as younger Rainbow folks often have a different set of values and priorities than their older Family members.

30. See the discussion forums on http://welcomehome.org/rainbow/index.html, accessed December 19, 2013.

31. Niman, *People of the Rainbow*, 115.

32. After policing the 2011 National Gathering in Washington state, Sheriff Dave Brown said, "You liken it to a small city. . . . You have a group of individuals that occupy this area in the national forest. With that comes everything you have in a city." Quoted in Smith, "More Than 10,000 Hippies Expected in Cherokee Forest by July Fourth."

33. Butterfly Bill, *Rainbow Gatherings*, 275.

Notes for Chapter 3

1. There is an events section on http://welcomehome.org/rainbow/index.html that lists most of the regional and international and all of the National Rainbow Gathering sites. Accessed December 19, 2013.

2. Andrew Abbott, *Department and Discipline: Chicago Sociology at One Hundred* (Chicago: University of Chicago Press, 1999), 197.

3. For example, Frederic Thrasher's *The Gang* is described by the very influential Chicago school sociologist Robert E. Park as a study not only of gangs but also equally of "'gangland'"—"that is to say, a study of the gang and its habitat." See Park, "Editor's Preface," in Frederic Thrasher, *The Gang: A Study of 1,313 Gangs in Chicago* (Chicago: University of Chicago Press, 1927). Another excellent example of Chicago school sociology's emphasis on spatial relations is Harvey Zorbaugh's *The Gold Coast and the Slum: A Sociological Study of Chicago's Near North Side* (Chicago: University of Chicago Press, 1929). See also Sudhir Venkatesh, "Chicago's Pragmatic Planners: American Sociology and the Myth of Community," *Social Science History* 25 (2001): 275–331.

4. Patricia A. Adler, *Wheeling and Dealing: An Ethnography of an Upper-Level Drug Dealing and Smuggling Community*, 2nd ed. (New York: Columbia University Press, 1993), 9.

5. Ibid., 63.

6. Georg Simmel, "The Stranger," in *Classical Sociological Theory*, 2nd ed., ed. Craig Calhoun et al., 295–299 (West Sussex, UK: Wiley-Blackwell, 2007), 296.

7. James Fox describing the settlement, or the spatial and organizational arrangement of territorial and familial units, "Translator's Introduction," in Marcel Mauss, *The Seasonal Variation of the Eskimo: A Study in Social Morphology* (London: Routledge and Kegan Paul, 1979), 7. Rainbow Gatherings are similar to the Eskimo settlement in that they are not permanent or definitely organized but rather spontaneously arranged based on common necessities and active participation in the arrangement and making of spatial organization, an organization that is simultaneously shaped by and shapes social interaction.

8. As Strauss et al. write, "the bases of concerted action (social order) must be re-constituted continually . . . 'worked at.'" See A. L. Strauss et al., "The Hospital and

Its Negotiated Order," in *The Hospital in Modern Society*, ed. E. Freidson (London: Collier-Macmillan, 1963), 147–169, 148.

9. Strauss et al. describe negotiated order as the "interplay of professionals and nonprofessionals—as professionals and nonprofessionals rather than just in terms of hierarchical position." Strauss et al., "The Hospital and Its Negotiated Order," 167. Similarly, people at a Rainbow Gathering act and interact as humans, all equally with a belly button. What people do in "Babylon" is irrelevant for how they'll be able to handle this negotiating process and participate in space-making at a Gathering.

10. Terry Williams, *Crackhouse: Notes from the End of the Line* (Reading, MA: Addison-Wesley, 1992), 42.

11. See Debra Mccown, "Rainbow Gathering Draws People from All 'Walks and Colors,'" http://www2.tricities.com/news/2012/jun/18/rainbow-gathering-draws-people-all-walks-and-color-ar-1994743/, June 18, 2012; Rain Smith, "More Than 10,000 Hippies Expected in Cherokee Forest by July Fourth," *Kingsport Times-News*, June 20, 2012; Nate Morabito, "Public Nudity an Issue during Rainbow Family Gathering," http://www2.wjhl.com/news/2012/jul/06/public-nudity-issue-during-rainbow-family-gatherin-ar-2039115/, July 6, 2012, accessed October 11, 2012; Allie Robinson, "Texas Tim: 'I Was Brought up Leaving the Place Better Than You Found It,'" http://www2.tricities.com/news/2012/jul/15/texas-tim-i-was-brought-leaving-place-better-you-f-ar-2057552/, July 15, 2012, accessed October 11, 2012; Roger Brown, "Rainbow Gathering Area in the Cherokee National Forest Almost Back to Normal," http://www2.tricities.com/news/2012/jul/31/rainbow-gathering-area-cherokee-national-forest-al-ar-2096192/, July 31, 2012, accessed October 11, 2012.

12. Strauss et al., "The Hospital and Its Negotiated Order."

13. Butterfly Bill has a rather harsh opinion of A-camp. He describes it as "a ghetto at the gathering, inhabited by a minority that most of the other gatherers looked down on, segregated so they could be quarantined." He notes that it's "located on the road so that was easy to go to the nearest town to buy more beer." Butterfly Bill [William S. Hirsch], *Rainbow Gatherings: A Memoir* (Muskogee, OK: Bliss Fire Press, 2010), 114. I disagree with both of these characterizations. While A-camp is certainly a louder, rowdier, and more violent space than Rainbow land, many of the folks I've met at Gatherings who don't themselves drink are sympathetic or even supportive of A-campers. Further, A-camp's location near the road serves a much larger function than simply easy access to beer; as even Butterfly Bill admits, A-camp's location helps it to serve as "a filter; drunken locals would stop at A-Camp instead of taking their carousing into the Gathering." *Rainbow Gatherings*, 115.

14. Michael Niman, *People of the Rainbow: A Nomadic Utopia*, 2nd ed. (Knoxville: University of Tennessee Press, 2011), 126.

15. As Butterfly Bill puts it, "At this end of the gathering one could truly have a week of spiritually uplifting activities, a lot of people's vision of an old time gathering,

without the need for ever going downtown." Butterfly Bill [William S. Hirsch], *Rainbow Gatherings, Volume Two: 2000–2012* (Muskogee, OK: Bliss Fire Press, 2013), 279.

16. Butterfly Bill, *Rainbow Gatherings*, 129.

17. Remember Andrew Abbott's remark about social organization, according to the Chicago school of sociology, as a process rather than a thing.

18. Hans Joas, *The Creativity of Action* (Chicago: University of Chicago Press, 1996), Chapter 3.

19. Strauss et al., "The Hospital and Its Negotiated Order."

20. Howard Becker, *Outsiders: Studies in the Sociology of Deviance* (New York: Free Press, 1991 [1963]), 196.

Notes for Chapter 4

1. See Max Weber, *The Essential Weber: A Reader,* ed. Sam Whimster (New York: Routledge, 2004), 138–142.

2. Butterfly Bill [William S. Hirsch], *Rainbow Gatherings: A Memoir* (Muskogee, OK: Bliss Fire Press, 2010), 124.

3. Ibid., 54.

4. Erving Goffman, *The Presentation of Self in Everyday Life* (New York: Overlook Press, 1959).

5. And not uphill from them, so rainwater doesn't flow down and contaminate.

6. Paul G. Cressey, *The Taxi-Dance Hall: A Sociological Study in Commercialized Recreation and City Life* (Chicago: University of Chicago Press, 1932), Chapter 3.

7. Some have certainly raised concerns about sanitation at a Gathering. See Melinda Wharton et al., "A Large Outbreak of Antibiotic-Resistant Shigellosis at a Mass Gathering," *Journal of Infectious Diseases* 162 (1990): 1324–1328; Centers for Disease Control and Prevention (CDC), "Public Health Aspects of the Rainbow Family of Living Light Annual Gathering—Allegheny National Forest, Pennsylvania, 1999," *Morbidity and Mortality Weekly Report* 49 (2000): 324–326; Robert M. Bossarte et al., "Injury, Violence, and Risk among Participants in a Mass Gathering of the Rainbow Family of Living Light," *Journal of Health Care for the Poor and Underserved* 19 (2008): 588–595.

8. Iddo Tavory and Yehuda C. Goodman, "'A Collective of Individuals': Between Self and Solidarity in a Rainbow Gathering," *Sociology of Religion* 70 (2009): 262–284.

9. Thomas F. Gieryn, "What Buildings Do," *Theory and Society* 31 (2002): 35–74.

10. Marcel Mauss, "Techniques of the Body," *Economy and Society* 2 (1973): 70–88.

11. Ibid., 84.

12. Ibid.

13. Ibid., 76.

Notes for Chapter 5

1. Quoted in Debra Mccown, "Rainbow Gathering Draws People from All 'Walks and Colors,'" http://www2.tricities.com/news/2012/jun/18/rainbow-gathering-draws-people-all-walks-and-color-ar-1994743/, June 18, 2012.

2. This chapter reviews the vocabulary and vernacular unique to the social world of a Rainbow Gathering, similar to Chapter 6 in Terry Williams's book *Crackhouse* titled "Lingo: Crackhead Trekkers Beaming Up." See Williams, *Crackhouse: Notes from the End of the Line* (Reading, MA: Addison-Wesley, 1992).

3. Erving Goffman, *Interaction Ritual: Essays on Face-to-Face Behavior* (New York: Pantheon, 1967), 41.

4. Ibid.

5. According to the Rainbow Family "mini-manual"—an ever-evolving and unofficial guide to life at a Gathering available at the information booth at every National Gathering and on the web at http://welcomehome.org/rainbow/index.html, "We have a tribal anarchy where we take care of each other because we recognize that we are All One."

6. Butterfly Bill writes, "Nowhere in Babylon did I hear people talking so much about food as I did at a Rainbow Gathering." Butterfly Bill [William S. Hirsch], *Rainbow Gatherings: A Memoir* (Muskogee, OK: Bliss Fire Press, 2010).

7. Goffman, *Interaction Ritual*, 17, note 11.

8. Butterfly Bill, *Rainbow Gatherings*, 210.

9. Victor Turner, *The Ritual Process* (London: Routledge and Kegan Paul, 1969), 167.

10. Georg Simmel, "Sociability: An Example of Pure, or Formal, Sociology," in *The Sociology of Georg Simmel*, ed. and trans. Kurt H. Wolff (New York: Free Press, 1950), 39–57.

11. As identified by Paul G. Cressey, *The Taxi-Dance Hall: A Sociological Study in Commercialized Recreation and City Life* (Chicago: University of Chicago Press, 1932), 31.

12. Emile Durkheim, *Elementary Forms of Religious Life* (New York: Free Press, 1995 [1912]).

13. Goffman, *Interaction Ritual*, 5.

14. Ibid., 23.

15. Simmel, "Sociability," 45.

16. Ibid., 52.

17. For, as Simmel tells us, conversation is "the most general vehicle for all that men have in common." Simmel emphasizes that "whatever the participants in the gathering may possess in terms of objective attributes—attributes that are centered outside the particular gathering in question—must not enter it." Ibid., 51. This is certainly true at a Rainbow Gathering, where people connect through communication not as members of a particular class, occupation, educational level, race, or any other outside characteristic but simply as a family of human beings connecting through communication.

18. Chris Shilling, "Embodiment, Experience and Theory: In Defence of the Sociological Tradition," *Sociological Review* 49 (2001): 327–344, 335. Shilling cites Durkheim, *Elementary Forms of Religious Life,* 213, 217.

19. This is a reference to communication with Forest Service or law enforcement, but power dynamics and conflict certainly enter some interactions among gatherers themselves.

20. Butterfly Bill, *Rainbow Gatherings,* 185.

Notes for Chapter 6

1. Quoted in Debra Mccown, "Peace Circle Highlights the Week for Those at Rainbow Gathering," *Bristol Herald Courier* (Virginia), July 5, 2012.

2. Erving Goffman, *The Presentation of Self in Everyday Life* (New York: Overlook Press, 1959), 20.

3. Erving Goffman, *Interaction Ritual: Essays on Face-to-Face Behavior* (New York: Pantheon, 1967), 20, 23.

4. Yet just like in Babylon, this may be especially true if they're a similar age, an opposite sex, attractive, and dressed in a way that appeals.

5. Michael Niman, *People of the Rainbow: A Nomadic Utopia,* 2nd ed. (Knoxville: University of Tennessee Press, 2011), 69. Here, Niman is referencing Rosabeth Moss Kanter's *Commitment and Community: Communes and Utopias in Sociological Perspective* (Cambridge: Harvard University Press, 1972).

6. Allie Robinson, "Many of the Rainbowers Are Professionals Who Just Come to Get Away," *Bristol Herald Courier* (Virginia), June 24, 2012.

7. Goffman, *Interaction Ritual,* 7.

8. Butterfly Bill [William S. Hirsch], *Rainbow Gatherings: A Memoir* (Muskogee, OK: Bliss Fire Press, 2010), 116.

9. Butterfly Bill [William S. Hirsch], *Rainbow Gatherings, Volume Two: 2000–2012* (Muskogee, OK: Bliss Fire Press, 2013), 22.

10. As Butterfly Bill puts it, "Whatever its nature, you gain honor and privilege thru [sic] your work, done right there at the gathering." *Rainbow Gatherings,* 345.

11. These three quotes reprinted from Rain Smith, "More Than 10,000 Hippies Expected in Cherokee Forest by July Fourth," *Kingsport Times-News,* June 20, 2012.

12. "Rainbow Festival Has Its Positives," http://www2.tricities.com/news/2012/jun/27/rainbow-festival-has-its-positives-ar-2015963/, June 27, 2012, accessed October 11, 2012.

13. W. I. Thomas, *On Social Organization and Social Personality: Selected Papers,* ed. Morris Janowitz (Chicago: University of Chicago Press, 1966), 133–139.

14. W. Lloyd Warner, "American Caste and Class," *American Journal of Sociology* 42 (1936): 234–237, 237.

15. See Niman, *People of the Rainbow*, Chapter 7, 131–147.

16. Tim Cahill, "Granby, Colorado, 1972: Armageddon Postponed," *Rolling Stone*, August 3, 1972.

17. Georg Simmel, "Sociability: An Example of Pure, or Formal, Sociology," in *The Sociology of Georg Simmel*, ed. and trans. Kurt H. Wolff (New York: Free Press, 1950), 39–57.

18. Butterfly Bill, *Rainbow Gatherings*, 230.

19. Talking about people getting high on marijuana at a Gathering, Butterfly Bill says, "The preponderance of people under the influence of this drug gave this assembly a different air from an affair where there are lots of people drinking alcohol." *Rainbow Gatherings*, 10.

20. Tim Olaveson, "Collective Effervescence and Communitas: Processual Models of Ritual and Society in Emile Durkheim and Victor Turner." *Dialectical Anthropology* 26 (2001): 89–124. Olaveson specifically references Victor Turner's *Dramas, Fields, and Metaphors: Symbolic Action in Human Society* (Ithaca, NY: Cornell University Press, 1974).

21. Mccown, "Peace Circle."

22. Robert K. Merton, *On Theoretical Sociology* (New York: Free Press, 1967).

23. Terry Williams, *Crackhouse: Notes from the End of the Line* (Reading, MA: Addison-Wesley, 1992), 41.

24. Butterfly Bill, *Rainbow Gatherings*, 29.

25. Quoted in Mccown, "Peace Circle."

26. As Mauss writes, "We might almost say that social life does violence to the minds and bodies of individuals which they can sustain only for a time; and there comes a point when they must slow down and partially withdraw from it. We have seen examples of this rhythm of dispersion and concentration, of individual life and collective life." Marcel Mauss, *Seasonal Variations of the Eskimo: A Study in Social Morphology* (London: Routledge and Kegan Paul, 1979), 79.

27. "Collective effervescence is thus characterized by intimacy, intensity, and immediacy, yet it involves will and intention, and symbolic focus. It is not simply mob psychology or camaraderie." Olaveson, "Collective Effervescence and Communitas," 101.

28. Erving Goffman, "The Interaction Order: American Sociological Association, 1982 Presidential Address," *American Sociological Review* 48 (1983): 1–17.

29. Goffman, *Interaction Ritual*, 5.

Notes for Chapter 7

1. See John G. Neihardt, *Black Elk Speaks* (Lincoln: University of Nebraska Press, 1972); Ed McGaa, *Mother Earth Spirituality: Native American Paths to Healing Ourselves and Our World* (New York: HarperCollins, 1990); Annie L. Booth and Harvey

L. Jacobs, "Ties That Bind: Native American Beliefs as a Foundation for Environmental Consciousness," *Environmental Ethics* 12 (1990): 27–43.

2. See Robyn Eckersley, *Environmentalism and Political Theory: Toward an Ecocentric Approach* (Albany: State University of New York Press, 1992).

3. See Arne Naess, "The Shallow and the Deep, Long-Range Ecology Movement: A Summary," *Inquiry* 16 (1983): 95–100; Bill Devall and George Sessions, *Deep Ecology: Living as if Nature Mattered* (Layton, UT: Gibbs Smith, 1985).

4. Bold and italics in original. A pdf of the mini-manual is available at http://welcomehome.org/rainbow/index.html, accessed December 19, 2013.

5. Technically, Forest Service regulations require that groups over a certain size sign a group camping permit. The Rainbow Family is against signing permits, because they are not an official organization and no one in their non-group has the right to sign for anyone else. The National Forest Service always has a huge attendance at the National Rainbow Gathering, with rangers and other law enforcement officials constantly present. Yet, although there is certainly tension at the bureaucratic level between these two groups, I've rarely seen it come through in interpersonal interaction. In my experience, most gatherers treat Forest Service rangers much like other attendees. They say "Welcome home" and "Lovin' you" to the rangers as they pass, and Forest Service rangers are mostly friendly, kind, and casual in their interactions with the gatherers.

6. From the Rainbow mini-manual, available at http://welcomehome.org/rainbow/index.html. Bold and italics in original.

7. Quoted in Michael Owens, "Java Fuels Rainbow Connection at Family Gathering," *Bristol Herald Courier* (Virginia), June 25, 2012.

8. "Rainbow Festival Has Its Positives," http://www2.tricities.com/news/2012/jun/27/rainbow-festival-has-its-positives-ar-2015963/, June 27, 2012, accessed October 11, 2012.

9. Data from Nate Morabito, "Public Nudity an Issue during Rainbow Family Gathering," http://www2.wjhl.com/news/2012/jul/06/public-nudity-issue-during-rainbow-family-gatherin-ar-2039115/, July 6, 2012, accessed October 11, 2012.

10. Texas Tim quoted in Allie Robinson, "Texas Tim: 'I Was Brought up Leaving the Place Better Than You Found It,'" http://www2.tricities.com/news/2012/jul/15/texas-tim-i-was-brought-leaving-place-better-you-f-ar-2057552/, July 15, 2012, accessed October 11, 2012.

11. Robinson, "Texas Tim."

12. Roger Brown, "Rainbow Gathering Area in the Cherokee National Forest Almost Back to Normal," http://www2.tricities.com/news/2012/jul/31/rainbow-gathering-area-cherokee-national-forest-al-ar-2096192/, July 31, 2012, accessed October 11, 2012.

13. At the 2012 National Gathering, I was one of them.

14. Quoted in Brown, "Rainbow Gathering Area."

15. Quoted in Robinson, "Texas Tim."

16. James Lovelock, *Gaia: A New Look at Life on Earth* (Oxford: Oxford University Press, 1979); James Lovelock, *The Ages of Gaia: A Biography of the Living Earth* (London: Bantam, 1990).

Notes for Chapter 8

1. Butterfly Bill [William S. Hirsch], *Rainbow Gatherings, Volume Two: 2000–2012* (Muskogee, OK: Bliss Fire Press, 2013), 20–21.

2. Erving Goffman, *Interaction Ritual: Essays on Face-to-Face Behavior* (New York: Pantheon, 1967); Randall Collins, *Interaction Ritual Chains* (Princeton, NJ: Princeton University Press, 2004).

3. See Collins, *Interaction Ritual Chains.*

4. Marcel Mauss says that most bodily techniques involve material tools. This could be a hammer, or a light switch, or a toilet, or myriad other things. See Mauss, "Techniques of the Body," *Economy and Society* 2 (1973): 70–88.

5. Emile Durkheim, *Elementary Forms of Religious Life* (New York: Free Press, 1995 [1912]); Victor Turner, *The Ritual Process* (London: Routledge and Kegan Paul, 1969).

6. Like they do at an arguably similar event, Burning Man. See www.burningman .com, accessed December 19, 2013.

7. In the translator's introduction to *Seasonal Variations of the Eskimo*, James Fox describes the relationship between material and cultural forms as one of "complex dependency" rather than "strict determinism" when explaining the paradigm underlying social morphology, or the attempt to explain the relationship between material, geographical, and technological systems and culture or forms of cultural expression. Fox, "Translator's Introduction," in Marcel Mauss, *Seasonal Variation of the Eskimo: A Study in Social Morphology* (London: Routledge and Kegan Paul, 1979).

8. Mary Douglas, "Symbolic Orders in the Use of Domestic Space," in *Man, Settlement, and Urbanism*, ed. P. J. Ucko, R. Tringham, and G. W. Dimbleby (London: Duckworth, 1972), 513–521, 514.

9. See R. E. Sclove, *Democracy and Technology* (New York: Guilford Press, 1995); Langdon Winner, "Do Artifacts Have Politics?," *Daedalus* 109 (1980): 121–136; Langdon Winner, *The Whale and the Reactor* (Berkeley: University of California Press, 1986).

10. See Winner, *The Whale and the Reactor*; Ulrich Beck, *The Risk Society: Toward a New Modernity* (Thousand Oaks, CA: Sage, 1992).

11. See Vance Packard, *The Waste Makers* (London: Longman, 1961); John E. Young, "Discarding the Throwaway Society," WorldWatch Paper no. 101 (Washington, DC: Worldwatch Institute, 1991); Zygmunt Bauman, *Society under Siege* (Cambridge: Polity Press, 2002).

12. Here, I am using alienation in the Marxist sense. See Karl Marx, *Economic and*

Philosophic Manuscripts of 1844, ed. D. J. Struik (London: Lawrence and Wishart, 1970); Bertell Ollman, *Alienation: Marx's Conception of Man in a Capitalist Society* (Cambridge: Cambridge University Press, 1971). See also John Bellamy Foster, "Marx's Theory of Metabolic Rift," *American Journal of Sociology* 105 (1999): 366–405; John Bellamy Foster, Brett Clark, and Richard York, *The Ecological Rift: Capitalism's War on the Earth* (New York: Monthly Review Press, 2010).

13. Turner, *The Ritual Process*, 177.

14. Paul G. Cressey, *The Taxi-Dance Hall: A Sociological Study in Commercialized Recreation and City Life* (Chicago: University of Chicago Press, 1932).

15. Ibid., 31.

16. Robert E. Park, "Editor's Preface," in Frederic Thrasher, *The Gang: A Study of 1,313 Gangs in Chicago* (Chicago: University of Chicago Press, 1927), x–xi.

17. Terry Williams, *Crackhouse: Notes from the End of the Line* (Reading, MA: Addison-Wesley, 1992), 1.

18. Ibid., 143.

19. Jane Addams, *Democracy and Social Ethics* (Chicago: University of Illinois Press, 1964), 9.

20. See John Stuart Mill, *On Liberty* (Boston: Ticknor and Fields, 1863).

21. See John A. Hostetler, *Amish Society* (Baltimore: Johns Hopkins University Press, 1993); Tom Schachtman, *Rumspringa: To Be or Not to Be Amish* (New York: North Point Press, 2006).

22. Michael Niman, *People of the Rainbow: A Nomadic Utopia*, 2nd ed. (Knoxville: University of Tennessee Press, 2011), 56.

23. See Mark Peyrot, "Narcotics Anonymous: Its History, Structure, and Approach," *Substance Use and Misuse* 20 (1985): 1509–1522; Javier Treviño, "Alcoholics Anonymous as Durkheimian Religion," *Research in the Social Scientific Study of Religion* 4 (1992): 183–208; Seán O'Halloran, "Power and Solidarity-Building in the Discourse of Alcoholics Anonymous," *Journal of Groups in Addiction and Recovery* 1 (2006): 69–95; Phoebus Zafiridis and Sotiris Lainas, "Alcoholics and Narcotics Anonymous: A Radical Movement under Threat," *Addiction Research and Theory* 20 (2012): 93–104.

24. At a meeting of one Christian kitchen, "women were told they should not go out into the rest of the gathering alone. If they were not with men, the sisters should always travel at least in pairs." Butterfly Bill, *Rainbow Gatherings, Volume Two*, 225.

25. Ibid., 287.

26. Durkheim, *Elementary Forms of Religious Life*, 425.

27. Butterfly Bill, *Rainbow Gatherings, Volume Two*, 42.

28. See Juliet B. Schor, *Plenitude: The New Economics of True Wealth* (New York: Penguin Press, 2010). Michael Niman makes a similar claim in the introduction to the revised edition of his book; he contends that farmer's markets and local food movements are examples of how Rainbow Family culture is entering the mainstream. While

I appreciate his optimism, I disagree with his claim (but not with the potential of such movements and practices).

29. Alternative communities come in all shapes and sizes, but there are some very successful examples of communities that demonstrate the ability to profoundly reorganize material and economic life based on sharing systems, such as Twin Oaks (http://www.twinoaks.org/), Acorn (http://www.acorncommunity.org/), East Wind (http://eastwind.org/), and Dancing Rabbit (http://www.dancingrabbit.org/). For a more comprehensive list of intentional communities of many different kinds across the United States, see the Fellowship for Intentional Community directory at http://www.ic.org/.

30. According to Howard Becker, deviance is *not* a quality of the act the person commits but rather a consequence of the application by others of rules and sanctions to an "'offender.'" Howard Becker, *Outsiders: Studies in the Sociology of Deviance* (New York: Free Press, 1991 [1963]), 9.

31. Patricia A. Adler and Peter Adler, "The Deviance Society," *Deviant Behavior* 27 (2006): 129–148.

32. See Mill, *On Liberty*.

33. Quoted in Debra Mccown, "Peace Circle Highlights the Week for Those at Rainbow Gathering," *Bristol Herald Courier* (Virginia), July 5, 2012.

Notes for Appendix

1. Michael I. Niman, *People of the Rainbow: A Nomadic Utopia*, 2nd ed. (Knoxville: University of Tennessee Press, 2011), Chapter 10 and epilogue 2.

2. Butterfly Bill [William S. Hirsch], *Rainbow Gatherings, Volume Two: 2000–2012* (Muskogee, OK: Bliss Fire Press, 2013).

3. My gender and the fact that I spent much of my time walking around with my partner also likely made it easier for me to interact with people in the parking lot and A-camp, where people are more likely to be vocally judgmental of others based on nonconforming appearances than people are in Rainbow land. Thank you to Butterfly Bill for reminding me of this.

4. Georg Simmel, "The Stranger," in *Classical Sociological Theory*, 2nd ed., ed. Craig Calhoun et al. (West Sussex, UK: Wiley-Blackwell, 2007), 295–299.

REFERENCES

Abbott, Andrew. *Department and Discipline: Chicago Sociology at One Hundred*. Chicago: University of Chicago Press, 1999.

Addams, J. *Democracy and Social Ethics*. Chicago: University of Illinois Press, 1964.

Adler, Patricia A. *Wheeling and Dealing: An Ethnography of an Upper-Level Drug Dealing and Smuggling Community*. 2nd ed. New York: Columbia University Press, 1993.

Adler, Patricia A., and Peter Adler. *Constructions of Deviance: Power, Context, and Interaction*. 5th ed. Belmont, CA: Thomson Wadsworth, 2006.

———. "The Deviance Society." *Deviant Behavior* 27 (2006): 129–148.

Anderson, Nels. *The Hobo*. Chicago: University of Chicago Press, 1961 [1923].

Bauman, Zygmunt. *Society under Siege*. Cambridge: Polity Press, 2002.

Beck, Ulrich. *The Risk Society: Toward a New Modernity*. Thousand Oaks, CA: Sage, 1992.

Becker, Howard. *Outsiders: Studies in the Sociology of Deviance*. New York: Free Press, 1991 [1963].

Booth, Annie L., and Harvey L. Jacobs. "Ties That Bind: Native American Beliefs as a Foundation for Environmental Consciousness." *Environmental Ethics* 12 (1990): 27–43.

Bossarte, Robert M., Ernest E. Sullivent III, Julie Sinclair, Danae Bixler, Thomas R. Simon, Monica H. Swahn, and Kristin Wilson. "Injury, Violence, and Risk among Participants in a Mass Gathering of the Rainbow Family of Living Light." *Journal of Health Care for the Poor and Underserved* 19 (2008): 588–595.

Bourdieu, Pierre. *Outline of a Theory of Practice*. Cambridge, UK: Cambridge University Press, 1977.

———. *The Logic of Practice*. Stanford, CA: Stanford University Press, 1990.

———. "Social Space and Symbolic Space." In *Contemporary Sociological Theory*, 2nd ed., edited by Craig Calhoun, Joseph Gerteis, James Moody, Steven Pfaff, and Indermohan Virk, 259–269. West Sussex, UK: Wiley-Blackwell, 2007.

———. "Structures, *Habitus*, Practices," in *Contemporary Sociological Theory*, 2nd ed., edited by Craig Calhoun, Joseph Gerteis, James Moody, Steven Pfaff, and Indermohan Virk, 270–289. West Sussex, UK: Wiley-Blackwell, 2007.

Bourdieu, Pierre, and Loic J. D. Wacquant. *An Invitation to Reflexive Sociology.* Chicago: University of Chicago Press, 1992.

Bourgois, Philippe. *In Search of Respect: Selling Crack in El Barrio.* Cambridge: Cambridge University Press, 2003.

Brewster, Bradley H., and Michael M. Bell. "The Environmental Goffman: Toward an Environmental Sociology of Everyday Life." *Society and Natural Resources* 23 (2010): 45–57.

Cahill, Tim. "Granby, Colorado, 1972: Armageddon Postponed." *Rolling Stone,* August 3, 1972.

Centers for Disease Control and Prevention (CDC). "Public Health Aspects of the Rainbow Family of Living Light Annual Gathering—Allegheny National Forest, Pennsylvania, 1999." *Morbidity and Mortality Weekly Report* 49 (2000): 324–326.

Collins, Randall. "From 'Stratification, Emotional Energy, and the Transient Emotions.'" In *Emile Durkheim: Sociologist of Modernity*, edited by Mustafa Emirbayer, 129–133. Oxford: Blackwell, 2003.

———. *Interaction Ritual Chains.* Princeton, NJ: Princeton University Press, 2004.

Cressey, Paul G. *The Taxi-Dance Hall: A Sociological Study in Commercialized Recreation and City Life.* Chicago: University of Chicago Press, 1932.

Cronon, William. "The Trouble with Wilderness: Or, Getting Back to the Wrong Nature." In *Uncommon Ground: Rethinking the Human Place in Nature,* edited by W. Cronon, 69–90. New York: Norton, 1996.

Desmond, Matthew. *On the Fireline: Living and Dying with Wildland Firefighters.* Chicago: University of Chicago Press, 2007.

Devall, Bill, and George Sessions. *Deep Ecology: Living as if Nature Mattered.* Layton, UT: Gibbs Smith, 1985.

Douglas, Mary. "Symbolic Orders in the Use of Domestic Space." In *Man, Settlement, and Urbanism*, edited by P. J. Ucko, R. Tringham, and G. W. Dimbleby, 513–521. London: Duckworth, 1972.

Durkheim, Emile. *Elementary Forms of Religious Life.* New York: The Free Press, 1995 [1912].

———. "The Dualism of Human Nature and Its Social Conditions," in *Emile Durkheim on Morality and Society*, edited by R. N. Bellah. Chicago: University of Chicago Press, 1973 [1914].

Eckersley, Robyn. *Environmentalism and Political Theory: Toward an Ecocentric Approach.* Albany: State University of New York Press, 1992.

Emirbayer, Mustafa. "Durkheim's Contribution to the Sociological Analysis of History." *Sociological Forum* 11 (1996): 263–284.

Fix, Alan G. "Fission-Fusion and Lineal Effect: Aspects of the Population Structure of the Semai Senoi of Malaysia." *American Journal of Physical Anthropology* 43 (1975): 295–302.

Foster, John Bellamy. "Marx's Theory of Metabolic Rift." *American Journal of Sociology* 105 (1999): 366–405.

Foster, John Bellamy, Brett Clark, and Richard York. *The Ecological Rift: Capitalism's War on the Earth.* New York: Monthly Review Press, 2010.

Fox, James. "Translator's Introduction." In *Seasonal Variations of the Eskimo: A Study in Social Morphology,* by Marcell Mauss. London: Routledge and Kegan Paul, 1979.

Gieryn, Thomas F. "What Buildings Do." *Theory and Society* 31 (2002): 35–74.

Goffman, Erving. *The Presentation of Self in Everyday Life.* New York: Overlook Press, 1959.

———. *Interaction Ritual: Essays on Face-to-Face Behavior.* New York: Pantheon, 1967.

———. "The Interaction Order: American Sociological Association, 1982 Presidential Address." *American Sociological Review* 48 (1983): 1–17.

Hirsch, William S. [Butterfly Bill]. *Rainbow Gatherings: A Memoir.* Muskogee, OK: Bliss Fire Press, 2010.

———. *Rainbow Gatherings, Volume Two: 2000–2012.* Muskogee, OK: Bliss Fire Press, 2013.

Hostetler, John A. *Amish Society.* Baltimore: Johns Hopkins University Press, 1993.

Joas, Hans. *The Creativity of Action.* Chicago: University of Chicago Press, 1996.

Kanter, Rosabeth Moss. *Commitment and Community: Communes and Utopias in Sociological Perspective.* Cambridge, MA: Harvard University Press, 1972.

Kohut, Mary. *Welcome Home: A Look into the Rainbow Family of the Living Light.* Self-published by author, 2008.

Lovelock, James. *Gaia: A New Look at Life on Earth.* Oxford: Oxford University Press, 1979.

———. *The Ages of Gaia: A Biography of the Living Earth.* London: Bantam, 1990.

MacLeod, Jay. *Ain't No Making It: Aspirations and Attainment in a Low-Income Neighborhood.* Boulder, CO: Westview, 2009.

Marx, Karl. *Economic and Philosophic Manuscripts of 1844,* edited by D. J. Struik. London: Lawrence and Wishart, 1970.

Mauss, Marcel. "Techniques of the Body." *Economy and Society* 2 (1973): 70–88.

———. *Seasonal Variations of the Eskimo: A Study in Social Morphology.* London: Routledge and Kegan Paul, 1979.

Mccown, Debra. "Peace Circle Highlights the Week for Those at Rainbow Gathering." *Bristol Herald Courier* (Virginia), July 5, 2012.

McGaa, Ed. *Mother Earth Spirituality: Native American Paths to Healing Ourselves and Our World.* New York: HarperCollins, 1990.

Merton, Robert K. *On Theoretical Sociology.* New York: Free Press, 1967.

Mill, John Stuart. *On Liberty*. Boston: Ticknor and Fields, 1863.

Naess, Arne. "The Shallow and the Deep, Long-Range Ecology Movement: A Summary." *Inquiry* 16 (1983): 95–100.

Neihardt, John G. *Black Elk Speaks*. Lincoln: University of Nebraska Press, 1972.

Niman, Michael I. *People of the Rainbow: A Nomadic Utopia*. 2nd ed. Knoxville: University of Tennessee Press, 2011.

O'Halloran, Seán. "Power and Solidarity-Building in the Discourse of Alcoholics Anonymous." *Journal of Groups in Addiction and Recovery* 1 (2006): 69–95.

Olaveson, Tim. "Collective Effervescence and Communitas: Processual Models of Ritual and Society in Emile Durkheim and Victor Turner." *Dialectical Anthropology* 26 (2001): 89–124.

Ollman, Bertell. *Alienation: Marx's Conception of Man in a Capitalist Society*. Cambridge: Cambridge University Press, 1971.

Owens, Michael. "Java Fuels Rainbow Connection at Family Gathering." *Bristol Herald Courier* (Virginia), June 25, 2012.

Packard, Vance. *The Waste Makers*. London: Longman, 1961.

Park, Robert E. "Editor's Preface." In Frederic Thrasher, *The Gang: A Study of 1,313 Gangs in Chicago*. Chicago: University of Chicago Press, 1927.

Peyrot, Mark. "Narcotics Anonymous: Its History, Structure, and Approach." *Substance Use and Misuse* 20 (1985): 1509–1522.

Ripley, Anthony. "Peace and Religious Festival Begins in Colorado," *New York Times*, July 2, 1972.

Robinson, Allie. "'Many of the Rainbowers Are Professionals Who Just Come to Get Away.'" *Bristol Herald Courier* (Virginia), June 24, 2012.

Schachtman, Tom. *Rumspringa: To Be or Not to Be Amish*. New York: North Point Press, 2006.

Schor, Juliet B. *Plenitude: The New Economics of True Wealth*. New York: Penguin, 2010.

Sclove, Richard E. *Democracy and Technology*. New York: Guilford, 1995.

Sentelle, David. *Judge David and the Rainbow People*. Washington, DC: Green Bag Press, 2002.

Shilling, Chris. "Embodiment, Experience and Theory: In Defence of the Sociological Tradition." *Sociological Review* 49 (2001): 327–344.

Simmel, Georg. "The Field of Sociology." In *The Sociology of Georg Simmel*, edited and translated by Kurt H. Wolff, 3–25. New York: Free Press, 1950.

———. "The Metropolis and Mental Life." In *Georg Simmel: On Individuality and Social Forms*, edited by Donald N. Levine, 23–34. Chicago: University of Chicago Press, 1971.

———. "Sociability: An Example of Pure, or Formal, Sociology." In *The Sociology of Georg Simmel*, edited and translated by Kurt H. Wolff, 39–57. New York: Free Press, 1950.

———. "The Problem of Sociology." In *Georg Simmel: On Individuality and Social Forms*, edited by Donald N. Levine, 23–34. Chicago: University of Chicago Press, 1971.

———. "The Stranger." In *Classical Sociological Theory*, 2nd ed., edited by Craig Calhoun, Joseph Gerteis, James Moody, Steven Pfaff, and Indermohan Virk, 295–299. West Sussex, UK: Wiley-Blackwell, 2007.

Siu, Paul S. P. *The Chinese Laundryman: A Study of Social Isolation*. New York: New York University Press, 1987.

Strauss, Anselm L. "A Social World Perspective." In *Creating Sociological Awareness*, edited by Anselm Strauss, 233–244. New Brunswick, NJ: Transaction Press, 1990 [1978].

Strauss, Anselm L., Leonard Schatzman, Danuta Ehrlich, Rue Bucher, and Melvin Sabshin. "The Hospital and Its Negotiated Order." In *The Hospital in Modern Society*, edited by E. Freidson, 147–169. London: Collier-Macmillan, 1963.

Tavory, Iddo, and Yehuda C. Goodman. "'A Collective of Individuals': Between Self and Solidarity in a Rainbow Gathering." *Sociology of Religion* 70 (2009): 262–284.

Thomas, William I. *On Social Organization and Social Personality: Selected Papers*, edited by Morris Janowitz. Chicago: University of Chicago Press, 1966.

Thrasher, Frederic. *The Gang: A Study of 1,313 Gangs in Chicago*. Chicago: University of Chicago Press, 1927.

Treviño, Javier. "Alcoholics Anonymous as Durkheimian Religion." *Research in the Social Scientific Study of Religion* 4 (1992): 183–208.

Turner, Victor. *The Ritual Process*. London: Routledge and Kegan Paul, 1969.

———. *Dramas, Fields, and Metaphors: Symbolic Action in Human Society*. Ithaca, NY: Cornell University Press, 1974.

Unruh, David. "Characteristics and Types of Participation in Social Worlds." *Symbolic Interaction* 2 (1979): 115–130.

Venkatesh, Sudhir. "Chicago's Pragmatic Planners: American Sociology and the Myth of Community." *Social Science History* 25 (2001): 275–231.

Warner, W. Lloyd. "American Caste and Class." *American Journal of Sociology* 42 (1936): 234–237.

Weber, Max. *The Essential Weber: A Reader*, edited by Sam Whimster. New York: Routledge, 2004.

Wharton, Melinda, Richard A. Spiegel, John M. Horan, Robert V. Tauxe, Joy G. Wells, Neil Barg, Joy Herndon, Rebecca A. Meriwether, J. Newton MacCormack, and T. H. Levine. "A Large Outbreak of Antibiotic-Resistant Shigellosis at a Mass Gathering." *Journal of Infectious Diseases* 162 (1990): 1324–1328.

Williams, Terry. *Crackhouse: Notes from the End of the Line*. Reading, MA: Addison-Wesley, 1992.

Winner, Langdon. "Do Artifacts Have Politics?" *Daedalus* 109 (1980): 121–136.

———. *The Whale and the Reactor*. Berkeley: University of California Press, 1986.

Young, John E. "Discarding the Throwaway Society," WorldWatch Paper no. 101. Washington, DC: Worldwatch Institute, 1991.

Zafiridis, Phoebus, and Sotiris Lainas. "Alcoholics and Narcotics Anonymous: A Radical Movement under Threat." *Addiction Research and Theory* 20 (2012): 93–104.

Zorbaugh, Harvey. *The Gold Coast and the Slum: A Sociological Study of Chicago's Near North Side*. Chicago: University of Chicago Press, 1929.

INDEX

✳ About the Author

Chelsea Schelly earned her PhD from the Department of Sociology at the University of Wisconsin–Madison and is assistant professor of sociology in the Department of Social Sciences at Michigan Technological University. Her work explores how the material, technological systems that support residential dwelling shape the organization of social life and conceptions of human–nature relationships. Her research examines the historical normalization of residential technological systems in America, how technological systems interact with social structures to shape human–nature relationships and human action, and how alternative technological systems challenge the political, economic, and environmental consequences of the currently dominant technological systems. She researches and writes about a diverse mix of alternative technological arrangements, including solar energy, living off-grid, intentional communities, and Rainbow Gatherings. She is interested in how alternative technologies and forms of material organization can reshape social organization in ways that benefit communities and the natural environment. She has participated in Rainbow Gatherings since she was seventeen years old.